SUCCESS.

Published by CelebrityPress®, Orlando, FL.

CelebrityPress® is a registered trademark.

Printed in the United States of America.

ISBN: 978-1-7334176-9-3
LCCN: 2020919520

Most CelebrityPress® titles are available at special quantity discounts for bulk purchases for sales promotions, premiums, fundraising, and educational use. Special versions or book excerpts can also be created to fit specific needs.

For more information, please write:
CelebrityPress®
520 N. Orlando Ave, #2
Winter Park, FL 32789
or call 1.877.261.4930

Visit us online at: www.CelebrityPressPublishing.com

SUCCESS.

CelebrityPress®
Winter Park, Florida

CONTENTS

CHAPTER 1

THE R-FACTOR: WHAT SUCCESSFUL PEOPLE DO DIFFERENTLY

BY JACK CANFIELD

Results transform the world.
Michael Gerber
Bestselling author of *Awakening the Entrepreneur Within:*
How Ordinary People Can Create Extraordinary Companies

Results. They're what help über-successful people achieve the extraordinary levels of success they enjoy in their lives. These achievers focus on results. And, in choosing this focused path, they follow a set of timeless principles that have been used throughout history by other successful people. When applied, followed and incorporated into your daily life, these principles can bring about the success you are seeking—and very often deliver better results than you ever imagined.

For more than 40 years, I've studied and used these principles to achieve incredible results in my own life. More than 15 years ago, I wrote a book called *The Success Principles* to catalog them for aspiring achievers everywhere.

So what are just a few of these core attitudes, habits, strategies and tactics that the world's top achievers use to get results in their careers, finances, lifestyle and more?

SUCCESSFUL PEOPLE FOCUS ON ACHIEVING LIFE-CHANGING RESULTS

Successful people don't always start with lots of money or high-level connections or other privileged circumstances, but they do stay focused on results that matter. They know which achievements will amplify and uplevel their life, and they stay focused on those accomplishing those goals. They research the steps, make plans, take action, and persevere until the results they want are achieved.

They Also Stay Focused on Their Core Genius

You have a unique ability or area of brilliance inside of you: something you love to do and do so well, it's effortless for you (and a whole lot of fun). If you could make money doing it, you'd make it your lifetime's work.

Successful people believe this, too. That's why they take the time to discover their unique brilliance, then put it first as a priority. They focus on it. And they delegate everything else.

Compare that to the rest of the world who goes through life doing everything—even those tasks they're bad at or that could be done cheaper, better and faster by someone else. They can't find the time to focus on their area of brilliance because they fail to delegate even the most menial of tasks.

When you delegate the things you hate doing or those tasks that are so painful, you end up putting them off, you get to concentrate on what you love to do. You free up your time. You become more productive and achieve more of the results you need. You get to enjoy life more.

Determine What You're Brilliant At . . .
Then Delegate Everything Else.

To help you determine your area of profound expertise (and those tasks you really should be delegating to others), follow the steps below. Keep in mind that you're looking for the one, two or three activities—your unique abilities—that not only bring you the most money, but that also bring you the most enjoyment and that you could spend all day doing.

Step One: Start by listing all those activities that occupy your time, whether they're business-related, personal, or related to your civic organizations or volunteer work. List even small tasks such as confirmation phone calls or paying bills.

Step Two: Choose from your list 1-3 things *that you are brilliant at*—things that very few other people can do as well as you.

Step Three: Next, choose those 1-3 activities from the previous list *that generate the most income* for you or your company.

Step Four: Circle individual activities that you selected in <u>both</u> *Step Two* and *Step Three* above. In other words, list activities that you are brilliant at *and* that generate the most income. These are the activities or areas of expertise where you'll want to focus the most time and energy.

Step Five: Name any "toxic" tasks from your original list in *Step One* that you especially dislike or that take too much of your time—activities you would gladly delegate to someone else if you could.

Step Six: Delegate those toxic tasks and less profitable activities. Find a capable person you trust, then delegate tasks *completely*. Explain the process fully and give 100% authority to accomplish the task in future, rather than delegating it each time it needs to be done.

SUCCESSFUL PEOPLE ARE SPECIFIC ABOUT THE RESULTS THEY WANT

Another reason why most people don't get the results they want is they haven't decided what those "results" are. They haven't defined their results—exactly—in clear and compelling detail. After all, how else can your mind know where to begin looking, seeing and hearing if you don't give it specific and detailed results to achieve?

> *The indispensible first step to getting the things*
> *you want out of life is this: decide what you want.*
> Ben Stein
> Writer, actor and social commentator

One of the easiest ways to begin determining what you truly want is to ask a friend to help you make an "I Wants" list. Have the friend continually ask, "What do you want? What do you want?" for 10-15 minutes, while jotting down your answers. You'll find at first that your "wants" aren't all that profound. In fact, most people usually hear themselves saying, *I want a sports car. I want a house on the beach.* But by the end of the 15-minute exercise, the real you begins to speak: *I want people to love me. I want to make a difference. I want to feel powerful*—wants that are true expressions of your core values.

Is "Making a Living" Stopping You?

Of course, what often stops people from expressing their true desire, is they don't think they can make a living doing what they love to do.

"What I love to do is hang out and talk with people," you might say.

Well, Oprah Winfrey makes a living hanging out and talking with people. And my friend Diane Brause, who is an international tour director, makes a living hanging out and talking with people in some of the most exciting places in the world.

Another woman once told me that her favorite thing to do was to watch soap operas.

"How can I make a living watching soap operas?" she asked.

Fortunately, she discovered lots of other people loved watching soap operas, too, but often missed their favorite shows because they also had to go to work. Being very astute, she created a little magazine called *Soap Opera Digest*. Every week, she watched all the soap operas, cataloged the plots and wrote up little summaries, so that if a viewer missed their soap operas that week, they would know who got divorced from whom, who finally married the doctor, and so on. Now she makes a fortune watching and publishing information about soap operas.

See how it's possible to make a great living doing what you want to do? You simply have to be willing to risk it.

Visualize What You Want

In addition to the "I Wants" list above, you can also decide what you want (and catalog it) through visualizing it. Have a friend read the following exercise to you (or audio-record it yourself in a slow, soothing voice, then listen to it with your eyes closed). If you record it, be sure to pause for a minute in between each category so you'll have time to write down your answers.

Begin by listening to some relaxing music and sitting quietly in a comfortable environment. Close your eyes. Then, begin visualizing your ideal life exactly as if you are living it.

1. First, visualize your financial situation. How much money do you have in your savings? How much do you make in annual income? What's your net worth? How about your cash flow?

2. Next, visualize your possessions. What does your home look like? Where is it located? What color are the rooms? Are

there paintings hanging on the walls? What do they look like? Walk through your perfect house visually, using your mind's eye.

At this point, don't worry about how you'll get that house. Don't sabotage yourself by saying, "I can't live in Hawaii because I don't make enough money." Once you give your mind's eye the picture, your mind will solve the "not enough money" challenge. Simply be honest with yourself about what you truly want.

Next, visualize what kind of car you're driving and the other possessions you own and enjoy. Open your eyes and write down what you see, in great detail. Or give your friend exact details to jot down.

3. Next, visualize your career. What are you doing in your career? Where are you working? Who are you working with? What kind of clients do you have? What is your compensation like? Is it your own business?

4. Then, focus on your free time and recreation. What are you doing with your family and friends in the free time you've created for yourself? What hobbies are you pursuing? What kinds of vacations do you take?

5. Next, visualize your body, physical health, emotional health, and spiritual life. Are you free and open, relaxed, in an ecstatic state of bliss all day long? What does that look like?

6. Then, begin visualizing your relationships with your family and friends. What is your relationship with your family like? Who are your friends? What are the quality of your relationships with friends? What do those friendships feel like? Are they loving, supportive, empowering? Could they be better?

7. What about your own personal growth? Do you see yourself going back to school, taking trainings, seeking therapy for a past hurt or growing spiritually?

8. Move on to the community you'd like to live in, the community you've chosen. What does your ideal community look like? What kinds of community activities take place there? What about your charitable work? What do you do to help others and make a difference? How often do you participate in these activities? Who are you helping?

Once you decide what you want in each of the eight areas above, you can begin to break down your lifestyle "wants" into small, achievable goals that will eventually bring about the life you want.

SUCCESSFUL PEOPLE SET GOALS THAT BRING ABOUT RESULTS

Extensive study has shown that—once we decide what we want—the brain actually helps us bring about these life-changing results. For instance, experts know that when you give it a goal, the brain triggers its *reticular activating system*—a web of neuro-pathways that filters through the millions of random images, facts and information we're bombarded with each day—then sends to our conscious mind those bits of data that will help us achieve our goals. When you give the brain an image of something you want to achieve, it will labor around the clock to find ways to achieve the picture you put there. Without a doubt, the brain is a goal-seeking instrument.

> *Goals are dreams with deadlines.*
> Diana Scharf Hunt
> Author of *The Tao of Time*

How Much By When?

Considering that your brain is working for you, it makes sense to be specific about your goals. When I teach about goal-setting, I stress the importance of setting goals that are both *measurable and time-specific.*

Measurable—The most powerful goals are those that are *measurable*, both by you and by others. For instance, your goal might be to generate a specific number of new clients for your new consulting firm so you can meet your income goals. By knowing the required number, you can focus on marketing campaigns, referral agreements and other systems that will hit that number.

Time-specific—Your goal should also be *time-specific*. In other words, not only should you state *how much* you'll earn, but also *by when* you'll earn it. Only with both these units of measure can you determine whether you've achieved your goal. You also become accountable to meeting your deadline.

Additionally, by being so specific, you can focus on the emotions you'll be feeling when you achieve your goal. Your brain then knows the payoff for hitting the target.

When you decide on the model of car you'll buy with your new-found income, the kind of house you'll live in, or which private schools your children will attend, you can't help but feel the positive emotions attached to those images. When you add emotion, color, detail, and features to visualizing your goals, your mind will begin in earnest to seek out ways to fulfill them.

A Breakthrough Goal Can Amplify Your Entire Life

Perhaps the true benefit of any goal is that—by pursuing it—you become a more confident, capable person. No one can ever take away the person you become as a result of pursuing your loftiest goals.

In addition to your many weekly and monthly goals, I recommend that you create *one single goal* such that, in the process of achieving it, you would uplevel every aspect of your life—from your finances to your friends, your business success, your lifestyle and more. Wouldn't that be a goal you would want to work on constantly and pursue with enthusiasm?

I call that a Breakthrough Goal.

For instance, if you were a consultant and you knew that you could land big tech companies as clients by speaking at the annual industry conference, wouldn't you work night and day to achieve that goal?

And if you partnered with smaller consulting firms to provide specific services that you can't do yourself, wouldn't that grow your business, your income, and your status in the industry— leading to other opportunities and a far more important network of connections than you have right now?

It would uplevel everything you do in your career and amplify who you are as a person. That's an example of a Breakthrough Goal.

SUCCESSFUL PEOPLE TAKE ACTION DESIGNED TO PRODUCE RESULTS

In the world today, most people are rewarded for action, not for ideas. Yet it's surprising how many people get caught up in planning, investigating and other preliminary activity when what they really should be doing is *taking action* on their goals.

When you take action, the Universe rewards that action with additional help that can speed you on your way. You also gain feedback about your chosen path or methods.

> *Things may come to those who wait,*
> *but only the things left by those who hustle.*
> ABRAHAM LINCOLN
> 16th president of the United States

The World Pays for What You Do, Not for What You Know

Many people have had good ideas—some of which led to entirely new industries or never-before-seen ways of making money. The Internet in its infancy was a place where many people had good ideas. But how many of those people took action and created the Google's, Amazon's, Facebook's and other businesses we know today?

The fact is that, while most people know *a lot* about making money or getting results or creating advancement in the world, only a few actually get to *enjoy the rewards* of this knowledge (whether financial, professional or otherwise) simply because the rest don't take action on their ideas.

Successful people, on the other hand, have a bias for action. More than any other characteristic, action is what separates the successful from the unsuccessful—the people who actually reap the rewards from those who would merely like to.

Perhaps you, too, had a great idea at one time—only to see it turned into a successful business or a new invention or a popular product *by someone else* because they took action and you did not.

The reality is that, in the world today, the people who are rewarded are those who take action. We're paid for what we do.

SUCCESSFUL PEOPLE ALSO RESPOND DIFFERENTLY TO GET BETTER RESULTS

One of the tenets I teach in my book *The Success Principles* is this equation:

$$E+R=O$$
Event + Response = Outcome

It's a powerful formula that demonstrates that every result or outcome (**O**) we get in life is a direct result of our response (**R**) to the countless events (**E**) that occur every day. In other words, whether our outcomes are financial success or financial scarcity, helpful relationships or disconnection, easy workdays or repeated frustration—all depends on the events that occur in our lives and how we respond to them.

Of course, how you respond is always your choice. You can choose to either blame the event—or you can take 100% responsibility for your response to it. Let's take a look:

Option #1: You can blame the event (E) for results you don't like (O).

What are some examples of events that can show up in anyone's life? A bad economy, workplace politics, an inattentive spouse, government or industry regulations, the city you live in, competition on the Internet, the fact that you have small children or aging parents to care for, and on and on. Many situations can't be helped; they just are. But if these situations were the deciding factor in whether someone was successful or not—no one would ever achieve anything.

Henry Ford would never have built the automobile, Margaret Thatcher would never have been elected Prime Minister, and Marc Andreeson would never have developed a way to browse the Internet. For every event that stops millions of people from getting what they want, hundreds of other people face that same event and succeed.

Option #2: You can decide to respond (R) differently the next time and automatically change the outcome (O) you get.

With this single decision, suddenly you'll begin to act with purpose. When faced with any event, you'll think consciously about your desired outcomes—then control your actions, behaviors and thoughts so they move you toward success instead of keeping you in victimhood.

After all, the only thing you really can change is your response to events—that is, how you accomplish your goals in spite of obvious roadblocks, lack of support, negative people in your life, and so on.

If you want better results or a better experience, you need only change your responses to the events that occur in your life. Change your thoughts of lack or helplessness into thoughts of abundance and action. Change the way you "see" yourself in your mind's eye to positive pictures of your exciting future with your own successful life. Change your non-productive activity into focused, consistent effort and productive work habits.

COUNTLESS RESULTS FROM SUCCESSFUL PEOPLE PROVE THESE PRINCIPLES WORK, IF YOU WORK THE PRINCIPLES

In the end, the results you enjoy in your life are a product of your habits, behaviors, thoughts and actions. When you become specific about the results you want—then set goals, take action, and focus on achieving them—your life will transform. You'll bring about the success and results you want.

By consistently acting upon these success principles, the only limiting factor will be your imagination and ability to dream about your future.

About Jack

Known as America's #1 Success Coach, Jack Canfield is the CEO of the Canfield Training Group in Santa Barbara, CA, which trains and coaches entrepreneurs, corporate leaders, managers, sales professionals and the general public in how to accelerate the achievement of their personal, professional and financial goals.

Jack Canfield is best known as the coauthor of the #1 *New York Times* bestselling *Chicken Soup for the Soul®* book series, which has sold more than 500 million books in 47 languages, including 11 *New York Times* #1 bestsellers. As the CEO of Chicken Soup for the Soul Enterprises he helped grow the *Chicken Soup for the Soul®* brand into a virtual empire of books, children's books, audios, videos, CDs, classroom materials, a syndicated column and a television show, as well as a vigorous program of licensed products that includes everything from clothing and board games to nutraceuticals and a successful line of *Chicken Soup for the Pet Lover's Soul®* cat and dog foods.

His other books include *The Success Principles™: How to Get from Where You Are to Where You Want to Be* (recently revised as the 10th Anniversary Edition), *The Success Principles for Teens, The Aladdin Factor, Dare to Win, Heart at Work, The Power of Focus: How to Hit Your Personal, Financial and Business Goals with Absolute Certainty, You've Got to Read This Book, Tapping into Ultimate Success, Jack Canfield's Key to Living the Law of Attraction,* his recent novel, *The Golden Motorcycle Gang: A Story of Transformation and The 30-Day Sobriety Solution.*

Jack is a dynamic speaker and was recently inducted into the National Speakers Association's Speakers Hall of Fame. He has appeared on more than 1000 radio and television shows including Oprah, Montel, Larry King Live, The Today Show, Fox and Friends, and 2 hour-long PBS Specials devoted exclusively to his work. Jack is also a featured teacher in 12 movies including *The Secret, The Meta-Secret, The Truth, The Keeper of the Keys, Tapping into the Source,* and *The Tapping Solution.* Jack was also honored recently with a documentary that was produced about his life and teachings, *The Soul of Success: The Jack Canfield Story.*

Jack has personally helped hundreds of thousands of people on six different continents become multi-millionaires, business leaders, best-selling authors, leading sales professionals, successful entrepreneurs, and world-class athletes while at the same time creating balanced, fulfilling and healthy lives.

His corporate clients have included Virgin Records, SONY Pictures, Daimler-Chrysler, Federal Express, GE, Johnson & Johnson, Merrill Lynch, Campbell's Soup, Re/Max, The Million Dollar Forum, The Million Dollar Roundtable, The Young Entrepreneurs Organization, The Young Presidents Organization, the Executive Committee, and the World Business Council.

Jack is the founder of the Transformational Leadership Council and a member of Evolutionary Leaders, two groups devoted to helping create a world that works for everyone.

Jack is a graduate of Harvard, earned his M.Ed. from the University of Massachusetts, and has received three honorary doctorates in psychology and public service. He is married, has three children, two step-children and a grandson.

For more information, visit:
- www.JackCanfield.com
- www.CanfieldTraintheTrainer.com

CHAPTER 2

SEVEN MARRIAGE SUCCESS STRATEGIES OF A CEO'S WIFE

BY JAIME LUCE

This week's headline reads that the gorgeous film star is marrying her handsome co-star. Next week's headline reads same couple is calling it quits. No one believes that a successful Hollywood or high-profile career marriage is possible. The myth is that to have a successful career means you can't have a successful marriage. You are either married to one or the other. That simply isn't true. It is possible to have both a successful marriage and an equally successful career.

Film stars Jessica Tandy and Hume Cronyn were married for 52 years until her death. Bill and Melinda Gates have been married for 23 years. Jeff Bridges and Susan Geston Bridges have been married for 45 years. Former President Jimmy Carter and his wife Rosalynn just celebrated their 74th anniversary.

My husband and I have been married for 26 years. He is a successful CEO for his two companies Previon and Bridgecom. After working outside the home for a time, I landed my dream job as a stay-at-home mom. No matter your profession, marriage works the same.

Happiness and longevity are not attributed to a contractual agreement or impressive pedigree. Marriage, like everything else in life, will rise or fall on the decisions and actions taken to build it and the tools and materials supplied by the builders. It will be as beautiful and enduring as you make it.

There is a wise saying that says, "Suppose one of you wants to build a tower. Won't you first sit down and estimate the cost to see if you have enough money to complete it?" Without a blueprint how can one build? Sadly, most couples spend time planning for the wedding but not for the marriage. They plan for a beginning and not for a lifetime. Marriage instead should be planned with the end in sight and then gather what is needed for its building. Without this investment you are sure to leave the project undone and never see its full fruition. In fact, doing this even before a spouse is chosen will determine the spouse you choose.

It was a Friday morning shortly after my wedding. My husband was getting ready for work and I was hurrying to get the kids off to school. We both ended up at the kitchen pantry at the same time with him looking for something to eat and me looking to see what to pack in the kid's lunches. As I stood holding each cabinet door open staring at the bare shelf, I heard these now unforgettable words. "Don't worry. It's Friday." I swung around with half a chuckle and half a glare and said, "I'm not your mom, honey. I don't go grocery shopping every Friday. I might. But I might not." We both laughed. He didn't even realize what he had said or what he was thinking. But this was a great aha moment for us. We decided to sit down and talk about our desires and expectations.

Our human nature is to mimic what has been modeled. How your parents modeled will affect your expectations in your marriage. Without realizing it, we all have unspoken expectations. "That's the way we did it in our house," may not be the way you did it in yours.

If your desire is to have both a successful career and a successful marriage, having the right strategy, a blueprint for building, will give you a head start.

STRATEGY NUMBER ONE

Set early boundaries of expectation and how that manifests for both of you.

Our first expectation was shared. We were in for life. We don't mention the word "divorce." An argument is simply a disagreement that needs hashing out and assumes you communicate. Those are just givens. But for a practical life example, my husband would handle all car issues, trash duty and the yard while I handled the house, meals and the kids. You need to understand and agree on who is responsible for what. There is no sense in needless petty misunderstandings. This is easy as long as both of you do what you promise to do. It also communicates respect and honor which frees you from frustration. Remember, it will be what you make it.

Discuss the expectations for family. If you have children, who takes them to school, rehearsals and practices? What are each of you expected to attend based off of your work schedule? If it is imperative that both parents are at every event, this must be hashed out prior to your children's participation in extracurricular activities. This could be a big bone of contention and it doesn't need to be. If one of your schedules doesn't allow for particular events everyone should already know this, so there is no disappointment for anyone.

We even used this with our children. Since we had four it was impossible for me to be in four different places at a time. My husband did not work close enough to get them here and there either, so we discussed how to work together. We decided that some seasons only one would be participating in a sport at a time. Or we found co-ed sports that they could do together. This of course is unique to each family dynamic.

A successful career can demand many extended hours of work. It is crucial to establish together and agree on how many hours away from home is acceptable and then stick to it. It is understandable that in every agreement the unforeseen can arise and you have to make a temporary adjustment. Just make sure that it is exactly that. Temporary. This rule applies to vacation time as well. What do you each expect? Family time that is uninterrupted and completely unhurried and enjoyable is critical for everyone. These times are for bonding and laughing and enjoying each other. During these times it's absolutely alright to be a bit selfish and expect your spouse not to give their time to work. And don't forget to have fun planning your fun. You can enjoy looking forward to your plans before your plans ever arrive.

STRATEGY NUMBER TWO

Take the time to understand one another's personalities.

Businesses wisely use the technique of having potential job candidates take a personality test. They need to see how they will respond with the team members already in place. The test can tell them how someone will respond under pressure and in predictable circumstances. It can mean the difference in a good hire or a quick fire. If this technique is a wise business practice, wouldn't it be even more valuable to really know the person you live with and want to build a long life with?

> The more you know about someone the more you can understand why they do what they do. It can make the difference when your spouse doesn't react the way you hoped for or you thought they would. When you understand someone, you have far more compassion for them. Taking the time to really know each other takes the sting out of potential issues.

In marriage you want your partner to be someone who shores up your weak spots. The reason we like to quote the old saying that two is better than one is because when one is down the other can pick them up. If opposites attract, we should know why. Human nature gravitates to what it isn't or doesn't have. It's appealing and usually desirable. The quiet one marries to bold one. The tall one marries the tiny one. We so easily tend to forget that the very trait that is driving you crazy right now was the thing that drew you to them to begin with.

When your differences arise, be a safe space to discuss them without accusing. Be willing to be honest about who you are, and not who you think you are based on who you want to be. Sometimes they are miles apart.

STRATEGY NUMBER THREE

Take an interest.

Learn each other's business to a degree that you can talk about it casually when with each other at the end of the day or when you attend business events or meetings together. People know you care because you take an interest in what they do and who they are while doing it. At a minimum, a career person will spend 40 hours a week doing a job. They spend most of their waking hours being that person. It's a huge part of who they are.

There have been many days I could tell by the look on my husband's face when he arrived home that it had been a rough day. I always ask about it. I want to be the ear that cares. To my husband's credit, I am asked on a regular basis what all I did that day, even though I don't work outside the home. He cares about what I am doing just as much I care about what he's doing.

Pay attention and ask questions. Know who their co-workers are. Know what the environment is that they work in every day. Our jobs are a way that we care for our families. We provide for the needs of the family through our jobs. Taking an interest says you are valuable and what you do is valuable.

STRATEGY NUMBER FOUR

Celebrate their success.

Be the cheerleader in every win regardless of whether it is big or small. When it's a big win make it a big deal! Your spouse should always be more celebrated at home than at the office. Tell the kids what a big deal their dad or mom is. Throw a party. Brag a little to your friends about them when they can hear you. Your enthusiasm will speak volumes.

During the climb of business there will be plenty of difficulties and sadly some losses, so never lose the great opportunity of a win. Never join the opposing team. When things aren't going well be resolved to be the encourager. Accentuating the positive will affect both of you for the good. We are told to never hang on to a drowning man or you'll both go down. Instead throw them a life preserver.

When my husband bought his first company we celebrated! We rented a room at a swanky restaurant with ocean views and invited all our friends to a huge dinner party. We flew in family from out of state and friends from out of the country. We made a lifelong memory. Your celebration may look very different and that's ok. Just celebrate.

STRATEGY NUMBER FIVE

Dream together.

A shared dream is a powerful partnership. It acts as a glue that keeps you together and going in the same direction. It costs nothing to dream and it stirs up many possibilities.

What will it take to get there? How long will it take? Plan what the steps are that you want to make towards it. Take turns in the drivers' seat. Sometimes one of you needs the focus for a while and at other times your spouse will need it. Like rowing a boat, you must row in sync to make headway or you'll just go in circles. If your dream has to be paused, dream a smaller or different dream in the meantime. Life happens but dreaming doesn't have to end.

STRATEGY NUMBER SIX

Let them play.

Everyone needs some 'me' time. Time for something fun, enjoyable and de-stressing. If it's golf they love, then encourage a game now and again. If it's brunch with friends, then put a date on the calendar. I don't mean to suggest that these happen so much that the family suffers, but they should happen. A full life breeds contentment. You will enjoy your marriage better together if you are allowed to enjoy being you. When your personal tank is full you will have more to give.

STRATEGY NUMBER SEVEN

Prefer one another.

My father-in-law always says, "you can't go wrong doing right." You will be faced with endless opportunities to choose yourself and how your feel. I challenge you to choose them instead. You got married to do life together. Marriage is a self-denying together edifying life. Selfish living produces lonely living. If it's all about you, you can be sure it is only your company you will keep.

> Be true to your promise. Remember the vision. Remember the best of each other and be the first to pull it out of one another. Show each other obvious mercy. They will be more apt to return the favor when it is you who needs it next time. Be ruthlessly committed. A marriage where each spouse continually chooses the other can't lose. You bring the building materials. The decision is always yours. Make a good one.

About Jaime

Jaime Luce is a sought-after author and speaker. Over the past two decades Jaime has served as a leadership and development pastor, teacher and blogger. She is a team-building and personal growth specialist. Her goal in every mode of ministry has been to empower others to discover the truth of who they are, while also equipping them to tap into God's abundant blessings.

Jaime attended The Kings University in Southlake Texas, with studies in Biblical and Theological studies.

Having grown up in a family who valued Christian Scripture and prayer, Jaime's faith in a real and personal God, is the foundation for all her communications. It remains her great joy to share and empower others with life-changing Bible truths.

With surprising and miraculous true-life stories, Jaime shares one of life's most powerful revelations in her upcoming book co-authored with her mother, Judy Mercer, titled, *You Don't Need Money; You Just Need God.*

Jaime and her husband own two companies in Yorba Linda, California, where they work alongside health care providers to meet the needs of their patients in the detection and prevention of Cancer.

Jaime resides in Newport Beach, California with her husband of 26 years, Joel. She considers her husband to be her greatest gift from God. The lasting and impactful lessons she has learned during their marriage served as the inspiration for her contribution to the book, *Success*, with author Jack Canfield.

Jaime believes her treasures in this life are their four adult children, their spouses, and their two adored grandchildren. Her favorite past time is spoiling them whenever possible.

CHAPTER 3

"NOT YOUR DADDY'S LAW FIRM"

BY CANDICE SHEPARD

The phrase "go big or go home" is kicked around quite frequently in my office. It's a reminder to us that we made a decision to do things a certain way and we're not going to compromise on the way that we've decided to do our work/run our business. I say "our" because even though my name is on the door, I'm never the most important person in the room. It's relational. I can do a lot of things, but I can only do what I can do. When I make my staff and my clients more important than me, on a fundamental level, that sentiment flows from me to them, and beautiful amazing things happen. The staff steps up and works harder, cares more, embodies and embraces my values and my vision and my plans for our office. The client settles in, breathes out, and becomes a lifelong fan. Why? Because we have properly cared for them. We have put the leader in a servant role and they know then that the leader can be trusted.

When I was in law school it was impressed upon us young, fresh-faced, hopeful about changing the world, future attorneys, that the prestige of the profession we were entering into created in us the ability to act a certain way, including the entitlement to be a pompous ass every chance we got. Not only *could* we act this way, but we *should*. It was a rite of passage and a requirement to being a good lawyer. It keeps the "others" in their places. You know, the other attorneys you were fighting against, the client who needs you more than you need them, the staff who only has a job because you are so amazing at yours. Getting out of school and entering the working world of the attorney, that sentiment was reinforced at every turn, especially by every 'old white guy' who called me sweetie and told me to step aside so he could work.

I was never very good at accepting that I needed to "step aside" and I had work of my own to do. So I embraced that 'old white guy' mentality and let everyone know that I was, in fact, the most important person in the room. I graduated at the top of my class from a top tier law school. I passed the Bar Exam on my first try. I was creating my own destiny by practicing law the way I wanted to. Nobody was going to step in and tell me what to do or how to do it. I stumbled along like that for a very long time. And I was a pretty good litigator. I made a lot of money, won a lot of cases, and had a lot of prestige.

But I was miserable. I hated my career and I hated my life. Not a great place to be at 28 years old. I stayed miserable for several more years, unnecessarily, making good money, winning a lot of cases, living in the "prestige." Then my husband got a job in another state and I had a chance at a reboot. I took a break from the law and from work in general, focused on my family, and spent a lot of time trying to figure out why the prestige and the money and the work were not enough and how I could make a change. I raised my babies and made new friends. I went back to church and found hobbies I enjoyed. I was no longer miserable at work, but I was not fully utilizing my degree and my brains and my work talent, so I was still a little miserable.

By societal standards, I think both of those phases could be considered successes for me. But for both of them, I was missing something.

I then went about a very strategic plan of figuring out what was missing. I didn't want to be a litigator any more. Every day, I felt like I was selling my soul to earn a living and clearly that wasn't working. So I decided on transactional work. I worked for several people for several years to learn a new type of law and glean information on what was working and not working in that particular industry. I worked for one man who ended up going to federal prison for embezzling a LOT of money from his firm, and another who was served with paperwork alleging tax evasion. That was the point I knew I could do better, so back out on my own I went.

Before going out on my own, I spent a lot of time praying about the type of business I wanted to create. I had the skill set to do the work, but the skill set to do the work and the running of the business itself are two very different animals. You'll find that as you're chasing success in your chosen field, you will have to be good at both. You'll also have to spend a considerable amount of time outlining your vision (what does success look like for you), your business plan (how will I get there), your budget (how will I pay for it). I contend, however, that the most important piece is your values. Be relentlessly faithful to the core values you hold for your life and you've got a great start.

For me, I knew going in that I wanted to serve the Lord in all that I did, love my clients with Biblical intensity, take care of my staff like family, and leave work at the end of the day knowing that I positively impacted the world. Pretty lofty goals, and very simple at the same time. It all comes down to service. I wanted to love people and serve them well. That may sound naïve in this day and age, and I had many tell me that I would fail with this as the lead goal in my company.

I walked in the door to my new business (don't get me wrong, scared to death), with a shiny new business plan saying I should be losing money for the first 18 months of being open – only to be profitable on the first day. I'd say that's success. The attitude of love and the mindset of service is where the magic happened.

Mahatma Gandhi once said, "The best way to find yourself is to lose yourself in the service of others." Could there be a higher calling? Whether you work in a service industry, or a production industry, or some hybrid of the two, any good business must have service at its heart. Stick with me here and I'll explain myself.

The Harvard Business School developed a core teaching module called the "service model", outlining an approach for crafting a profitable service business based on four critical elements. (I argue that this also applies to a product-based business model, as service is essential to every business success.) < https://hbr.org/2008/04/the-four-things-a-service-business-must-get-right >

According to Harvard, a business must have four core elements:

1. **The Offering:** The challenge here is that management needs to make a decision about what the ideal customer of the business will desire and focus attention there. For my business, that decision was to provide excellent service, friendliness, convenience, and comfort. The tradeoff is that we're not the cheapest option in town. Our customers are ok with that because they prefer the tradeoff.

2. **The Funding Mechanism:** "Excellence comes at a cost and the cost must ultimately be covered." This can be accomplished in a variety of ways, from simply having the customer pay for it through extra costs associated with the service, to adding value in the form of intangibles that justify the extra costs. Or, even by finding "ways to enhance the customer experience even while spending less."

3. **The Employee Management System:** in my field, as with most service-based industries, and I cannot stress this enough, who you have on your team will make or break you. *Spend the time to recruit, select, train and retain the best talent with the attitude and mindset that builds the brand your company is seeking to propagate.* Anything less is certain death to the company.

4. **The Customer Management System:** "Service designs may call for customers to perform important tasks," or at a minimum, to have a certain amount of input. But those customers don't have to interview or submit to a background check to qualify. In managing customers in your operations, then, you may have to make some difficult decisions. I once had a boss who told me he rarely regretted firing a client, but he frequently regretted keeping some of them. So choose wisely.

With those four core elements in mind, let's break it down to some nitty gritty. I love the quote by Ralph Waldo Emerson in which he said, "The purpose of life is not to be happy. It is to be useful, to be honorable, to be compassionate, to have it make some difference that you have lived and lived well." If you can be all those things, you WILL be happy, and therefore SUCCESSFUL.

Remember, the goal here is to love people and to serve them well. With that in mind, what does really good service look like? The kind where your clients and customers are happy to walk into your office, and even happier when they walk out? It comes back to that concept of loving people. They need to walk in and feel the love. That's why my business is "not-your- daddy's-law-firm." There is not a bit of ego or mahogany or pompousness. I am always the least important person in the room, and I am always showing up with love and a servant's heart. I hire people with the same mindset as well. Here are some examples of things that are working really well for us:

I. No one can be all things to all people. Choose what you'll do, and do it really, really well. Choose how you're going to do it and remember that the customer will always remember how you made them feel. As attorneys, we have the legal and (theoretically anyway) the skill set to practice any type of law we would like to practice. We do two things in my office. And we have honed and refined the systems and processes and knowledge base in which to do those two things, and we are therefore very good at those two things. If a case walks through our door that we're not competent to handle, we refer it off to someone who is competent to handle it. We lose the revenue from that one client, but we don't risk our reputation and our sanity, and perhaps even our ability to practice law altogether, by engaging in something in which we are less than stellar.

II. When you mess up, or someone on your staff messes up (we're all human, it's going to happen), OWN IT <u>AND FIX IT!</u> Make sure your staff knows what happened, where the breakdown occurred, and how you chose to fix it. But never humiliate them and always let them know you've got their back. And again, the buck stops with you, Boss Lady (or Boss Dude). Regardless of what happened, it's yours to own. Make sure you fix it in such a way that:

(a) everyone on your staff is aware of how to avoid that mistake in the future, if possible.
(b) your client walks away feeling whole, heard, and appreciated.

III. Which leads into this: serving well and saying no don't go hand-in-hand always, but they do have to coexist. My suggestion is to never say "no" outright. Listen fully to the problem and the request and ask for some time to reflect on it. When you go back to the client or the staff member with a "no", or even a "yes, but" be gentle and kind, and always give a little more than you're comfortable with. Don't give away the farm, obviously, but do be willing to take a hit for the sake of the relationship. (Remember I started this with "you've got to love people." This is where the rubber meets the road. And it can be HARD.)

IV. Nurture the relationships. All the relationships. The ones who bring you business, and the ones who clean the bathrooms. The ones who are "important" and the ones who are not. Greet everyone who walks in the door or calls on the phone as if they are the most important person you'll talk to that day. Smile, shake hands (when global pandemics don't prohibit it), hug if you're so inclined, ask about the family and their weekend. Celebrate their wins and help them resolve their challenges. Your business will grow exponentially, but you'll also sleep really well at night.

V. Make your place of business inviting. Who has ever gone into a building or an office or a store and felt immediately stifled? That's not a great first impression. Make sure your space is well lit, inviting and clean, that it smells good and looks good in a homey kind of way. Offer snacks and drinks. Make sure your clients know that you and your staff are glad they've chosen you. Figure out how to have a conversation with the client that eases their discomfort. [Hint: "I'm an introvert" is not an excuse here.] Your name is on the wall so you have to get out of your own way. Laughter is always a good idea. And don't forget to be grateful. I end every transaction with "thank you for letting us help" and "please let us know what else we can do for you."

MEASURING SUCCESS

The measure of success is largely dependent on what your definition of success looks like. But I think the one thing that is universal is that you have to be true to your values and the vision that you've set up for the success in your life. The minute you stray from matching your values to your business life you lose a large piece of who you are and what you stand for. Then any definition of success is long gone. You can get it back. But start with love. Let love lead and you'll be successful no matter what your definition of success looks like.

About Candice

Candice Shepard wears many hats, and loves them all. Jesus-lover, wife, mother, sister, daughter, orphan advocate, animal rescuer, and friend are her favorites. She also proudly wears the hats of attorney, entrepreneur, thought leader, influencer, mentor, speaker, author, and servant leader.

A native of the Midwest, Candice grew up in a very small town, daughter to a locomotive engineer and a teacher, played lots of sports and graduated with a class of 28 students, most of whom she had gone to kindergarten with. Her parents were at every game and academic event and the value of hard work, education, humor, and service to others were firmly ingrained in her upbringing. She joined the Army National Guard at the age of 17 to earn money for college and then earned a Bachelor of Arts in Communications from the University of Illinois (Go Illini!) and a Juris Doctorate from the University of Iowa (Go Hawks!). She now proudly calls North Carolina home along with her husband, four children, and menagerie of fur babies. That Midwestern pragmatism is still very much present in her parenting, daily living, and business.

Candice is the CEO and Managing Attorney of Shepard Law, PLLC, a law firm in the Charlotte, NC Metro area serving multiple counties in two locations. The firm's revenue and client base has doubled and tripled year-over-year by prioritizing the service philosophy at the forefront of the business model, and seeking out a unified team who have the same mindset.

Candice is also the Founder and the President of the Board of Directors of Tribe 14:18 Ministries, a nonprofit being brought to fruition out of the desire of Candice and some of the most amazing Mamas on the planet who seek to care for orphans and the families who love them. Finally, Candice is a certified Canfield Success Principles Trainer and international speaker with The Athena Tribe. Candice seeks to empower others in all aspects of life and her diverse endeavors are driven by that desire.

Candice also loves to connect!
- www.ShepardLawPLLC.com
- www.Tribe1418.com
- www.TheAthenaTribe.com

CHAPTER 4

DO IT TODAY: THE IMPORTANCE OF CLARITY AND CONFIDENCE IN ACHIEVING YOUR DREAMS

BY ALEXANDRA ALLEN

I believe we need to lead, educate, and inspire the world with media.
~ Nick Nanton

INTRODUCTION

Some years ago, I attended the Women's Economic Forum, where women from around the world gathered to discuss issues regarding leadership, business, government, and policies. The committee of the Women's Economic Forum asked me to be part of a panel so I could share my passions of humanitarian documentary films and Latin classics studies. I love Latin classical studies because the classical world of Ancient Rome and Greece has many lessons that apply today to my life. I love documentary films because they bring awareness to issues that need to be told to better the world we live in.

I was motivated in Latin classical studies and documentary films because I am passionate about these topics. Through accomplishments as a filmmaker and classicist, I was able to identify steps to take for success that apply to life. I established clear goals, created specific plans with daily review, identified areas to specialize, acted quickly, practiced, improved daily, and sought mentorship from successful people and experts. Here are the biggest lessons I have learned.

CLEAR GOALS GIVE YOU SOMETHING TO SHOOT AT

The trouble with not having a goal is that you can spend your life running up and down the field and never score.
~ Bill Copeland

1. Set Goals: The first step is knowing what you're shooting at because you can't hit a target you can't see. Unless you know where you're headed, the stream of life takes you wherever it wants. Identifying goals is paramount to success, whatever your definition may be. Your dreams are only figments of imagination unless clearly written as goals. For example, I wanted to succeed in Classical Studies and Latin. I then defined what success would look like: competing successfully in Certamen competitions, leading Latin leagues, and conducting independent research. I then clarified these goals by talking with people who were experts in the subject. By being clear on these goals and writing them down, I was able to accomplish them and not waste time on less important activities that would not get me to where I wanted to go.

First, sit down at a table and take out a paper and pen. Then think about what you envision as success in different areas of your life. These areas could be health and energy, work, relationships, eternal destiny, and financial. Health and energy describe physical and mental wellbeing; work describes your everyday tasks that have a special meaning; relationships refers to emotional health and the people close to you; eternal destiny refers to religion or spirituality, and financial refers to financial independence separate from work. Create at least three goals in each of these areas that you envision as successful.

These goals should be long-term, clear, quantifiable, time-bound and written in the present tense. For example, if I wanted to set a clear and quantifiable health and energy goal, I could set a goal of running a half-marathon. I would set a deadline and write the goal in the present tense, so I would say, "I run a half-marathon in two hours by April 1." This goal is not vague and can be clearly accomplished. Also, by setting a date, the goal seems more realistic. Lastly, writing in the present tense gives you the sense that you are perfectly capable of reaching this goal. Using these criteria, you should come up with a list of about 15 goals. While these goals can be more long-term, you should revise your master list of goals every time you accomplish a goal or every month.

PLANNING AND REVIEWING DAILY KEEPS GOALS PRESENT AND GIVES A CLEAR ROADMAP

The successful warrior is the average man, with laser-like focus.
~ Bruce Lee

2. Specific Plan and Daily Focus: After making clear goals and writing them down, you must prioritize them by importance and sequence. Prioritize the goals that will have the most impact on your success, labeling the goals with letters "A" through "D", and then number each goal within each letter category. Then, starting with "A1", create a clear plan with smaller goals ordered sequentially for each of your goals. For example, after prioritizing all my goals, I would go down the lettered list, number in each category, and create a plan for each goal; for the half-marathon goal, I would create a plan of finding and registering for a half-marathon, training daily, eating a healthy diet, and sleeping at

43

least eight hours nightly. A detailed plan is paramount to achieving these goals because it provides a clear roadmap that helps you focus on achieving smaller goals instead of being overwhelmed by a seemingly impossible large goal.

Keep your goals in plain view to review daily. Put the list on your bathroom mirror, on the wall above your desk, or even as your home screen. This daily review keeps goals in your subconscious and allows you to constantly seek and take advantage of opportunities that bring success in your areas of interest. I have always loved documentary films as they transported me to a new reality, and I wanted to be part of producing some. So, after many years, when I saw the opportunity to co-produce a documentary film on PTSD in US military veterans and canines that help them overcome this trauma, I immediately jumped on it and immersed myself in the idea and details of how dogs help veterans. If I had not set this goal and kept it present, the opportunity would have passed by.

SPECIALIZE IN NICHE AREAS THAT GIVE YOU A COMPETITIVE ADVANTAGE

Each man is capable of doing one thing well. If he attempts several, he will fail to achieve distinction in any.
~ Plato

3. **Specialize:** Specializing and mastering a niche gives you an edge instead of being somewhat skilled at many aspects. Instead of trying to learn everything about the classical world, I focused on ancient Rome, mastering its history and language. This allowed me to do well in niche competitions and national exams. Identify an area that interests you and you could master. Likewise, film is broad, so I chose documentary films that have a humanitarian purpose surrounding US military veterans because my grandparents served in the two World Wars and because I know many military veterans in my community.

In your areas of interest, explore different fields that you find interesting. You could study a certain discipline, take a course, or do an internship. After delving into different spheres, choose one that you could master and that could be your niche. While you should be comfortable with the other aspects of this interest area, zero in on the aspect that makes you a superstar. Become a master in this niche through continual learning and practice. Be self-motivated and seek new opportunities through the internet and connections, and then create independent projects that showcase your expertise in your niche. When you become so unique, you make your own class.

SEEK MENTORSHIP FROM EXPERTS

Surround yourself with those who only lift you higher.
~ Oprah Winfrey

4. <u>**Associate with Successful People and Mentors:**</u> Connecting with successful people in your field is key in improving and creating opportunities. By associating with experts, you can learn and gain new insights. For example, Kevin Perry, Katharine Sheeler, Sarah Lannom, Cindy Calder, Nick Nanton, Ramy Romany, Carlo Orecchia have all modeled and helped me in the development of my passion for Classical studies and documentary films. They encouraged and opened opportunities for me to further my knowledge and lead me to new experiences. Some have led me to new countries, new studies, new ways of working, giving me advice, supporting me, being a role model, striving to make a difference, encouraging me to believe in impossible goals and being conscious about details of my craft.

Find people already successful in your field and continue reaching out—asking for advice and learning from their work. Email or connect with experts offering or giving something that would help them. Sacrifice your time and energy in exchange for experience and expert advice. This mentorship is worth so much more than immediate possible monetary gain.

ACT, ACT, ACT

Action is the foundational key to all success.
~ Pablo Picasso

You don't have to be great to start, but you have to start to be great.
~ Zig Ziglar

5.   Act Quickly: Knowledge without action is useless. If you had all the knowledge in the world, but don't use it, it's as if you had none at all. Once you've established goals and clear action plans, start. Follow your action plans making intentional steps towards your goals because movement is not the same as progress. Sitting in a rocking chair allows for movement but no forward progress. Don't confuse movement with progress. Additionally, don't wait too long or the opportunity escapes you. I learned this lesson when registering for Latin competition exams. After identifying tests that I wanted to take, I made the mistake of putting the list away without checking the registration deadlines and making action plans for these tests. After a few weeks, I happened on the list and realized I had only a few days to register. Luckily, I was still able to register for exams but if I had waited a few days later, I would have missed the annual deadline. While I learned this lesson in a small way, this idea is crucial.

Usually, we procrastinate because fear of failure stems from a fear of others' opinions. People make excuses that it's not the right timing, that they don't have the right connections or resources, or simply that they are incapable of accomplishing their goals. Understand that no one else is responsible for your success or failure. Lisa Nichols said, "Mostly, the world sees you the way you see yourself." Until you take ownership of your life and realize that you are capable, you are imprisoned by your own mindset. Don't wait before it's too late, ACT!

DAILY PRACTICE FOR MASTERY

We are what we repeatedly do. Excellence, then,
is not an act but a habit.
~ Will Durant

6. <u>**Continuous Improvement:**</u> To stay on top of your area of expertise, you must constantly learn from the best, analyze your past actions and projects, and expand your knowledge. The Japanese have captured this concept with the word "kaizen" meaning continuous and never-ending improvement. Information is always being discovered so you must continuously update your knowledge. There is always more to learn. Take courses, connect with other experts, and keep practicing your trade.

I continue to take new film courses learning about improving technology in editing, cinematography, and production. I associate with film experts and understand their views as well as watch documentaries that amplify my perspective. Additionally, I practice my craft daily by staying updated on new technology and techniques. The more I learn, the more I realize that there is so much I don't know. Continual practice and reflection allow for improvement of my skill.

CONCLUSION

When your clarity meets your conviction and you apply action to
the equation, your world will begin to transform before your eyes.
~ Lisa Nichols

As I stepped off the stage at the Women's Economic Forum, I realized the importance of these opportunities. Because these are gifts, I feel obligated to make a contribution where I see room to help, using lessons from the Classics and documentary films.

Ultimately, you decide your success if you never give up. So I encourage you to continue onward and upward. Set goals, focus daily, specialize, get mentors, act quickly, and continuously find ways to improve. These steps were taught to me, and through my own trial and error, I learned to apply them. Clarity in your goals and confidence in your capabilities are paramount to achieving what you've always dreamed of.

SO DREAM BIG AND BE THANKFUL

About Alexandra

Alexandra Allen is at the National Cathedral School located on the campus of Washington's National Cathedral, and thrives on high expectations and good judgment. She has lived with her family in Guadalajara, Beijing (where she attended the British School), New York City (where she attended the Brearley School), and Washington D.C. (where she attended Sidwell Friends School), and enjoys Latin classical studies and humanitarian documentary films.

She has drawn national recognition, being awarded the *Young Leaders Award* by the Women's Economic Forum, an *EXPY* Award for media and communications, and has co-produced film documentaries – which have won six *Emmy* Awards, multiple *TELLY* Awards, a *Quilly* Award, and is a Best-Selling Author.

Among the documentaries are:
- *K9's for Warriors* – about Post Traumatic Stress Syndrome among U.S. military heroes and the service dogs that help them.
- *Folds of Honor* – about college scholarships for children of deceased war heroes.
- *It's Happening Right Here* – about the fight against sex trafficking that affects Latino children in the US.

In addition to Classics, she enjoys advanced math and science, having won an academic Valedictorian award. She studies Latin language and History, tutors students in Latin, and leads the Latin Certamen Club which investigates Classical culture. Independently, Alexandra conducts Classics research around how films portray Ancient Rome, and is a founder of the Washington, D.C. Chapter of the Junior Classical League. As a member of the NCS Film Club, she started *La Perspectiva*, a newsletter for Latino Students, and serves as head of film news for NCS's newspaper. Currently, she is working on programs that empower Latinas in documentary film.

From childhood, she has traveled to over 12 developing Latin American countries on Vision Trips, helping to raise funds through film, bringing awareness and culture-language translation for orphanages and childrens' feeding centers where vulnerable girls are protected, taught values and work skills, and educated to improve their futures. She has witnessed firsthand while working overseas with girls, that their future is one they can be empowered to improve. Alexandra believes that wherever she finds injustice and need, she has a responsibility to encourage and help.

Contact information for Alexandra:
- Email: alexallen940@gmail.com
- Phone: (757) 912-3252

CHAPTER 5

BELIEF, FEAR AND THE OUTCOME

BY ANDY MCGLYNN

"Hi, I'm Andy your new PT". These were the first words out of my mouth as I arrived for the first day of what wasn't just to be my new job, but the first day of the rest of my life and the extraordinary journey it has taken me on…which, incidentally, has brought me all the way to speaking to you right now.

The response was not what I was hoping or expecting… *"Huh, PT, won't work here. Good luck with that, mate"*. This was followed by the individual about-turning and walking off in the most blatant fashion I think I've ever seen.

Fast forward some 24 months later, and not only did I have a personal PT business of 130 hours a month of PT at $50, but I also had 10 other PT's working for me and had just been asked at the tender age of 25 to start travelling to other gyms to teach other Personal Trainers to grow and build their business. Life just suddenly went on fast- forward, and I ran with the ball.

What got me through? Refusal to act on my fear, which in the early days was probably more because of naivety, and a surging, unshakeable and unequivocal belief. Did I feel the fear? Yes, of course! For nine months I woke every morning convinced my client base would dry up. But just think about that for a moment, does that sound rational? Of course not. Maybe clients would drop off within an assumed and accepted attrition rate, but there wouldn't just be that one day in which my entire client base woke and decided they were going to cancel my services. So, what was going on here for me? Well, probably the same as what goes on for you when something is going so well for you that it starts to challenge the results you've come to expect. The ego starts presenting you with suggestions, and the more creative you are, the more grandiose those suggestions that the ego is able to conjure. It's using your own extreme creative gene, the same one you've used to build your business or create an idea, it's using it against you to make these unfounded, outlandish suggestions. I think this is why people created the acronym of F.E.A.R...

"F.E.A.R. – FALSE EXPECTATIONS APPEARING REAL"

I didn't create this, so I can't take credit for it, but isn't it so true? What rationale and statistics does fear really have to back these thoughts up, which we all allow to stand in the way of progress? None of course, which suggests they've come from another place, perhaps a growth from another unhealthy belief that you may carry about your world.

Looking back, I now realise and wish to articulate to you that you're never going to stop limiting beliefs creeping in. Everybody has a threshold of what they can cope with when it comes to certainty and security, you've probably seen it on game shows when the contestant is offered to gamble with what they have won so far on the show, and I find it fascinating to see those who take the risk and those who don't. What happens is a gradual shift from making decisions based from 'within' to the decision being formed on information from 'without', in other words – factors outside of them. As soon as those factors outside of you start to creep into your decision making, you let the programme of fear 'run riot' once it gets in.

I don't know how else to say it to you. You have to stay 'within'. The answers are always going to be found inside you, we don't know just how much power we really have, the leading specialists in the field of 'the mind' still can't quantify or measure the limitations. We are dealing with something beautifully invisible, but tangible at the same time; the tangibility comes from the results we are able to show. In every case, our results are merely a representation of our thinking, and our words also advertise and give away our limitations.

Come back to that decision the game show contestant makes; it's always from outside of them. "I've had a lovely day, it's a lot of money, we came with nothing and we've now won $x's, my wife will kill me if I get the answer wrong, I'm just not sure… so, I think…I'm not sure, no I am sure, I'm going to take the money". This final ending of the decision is always a result of intuition and fear fighting it out. The mind trying to go back within and find the answers, the courage and the truth inside of itself, but the noises from all those powerful externalisations often win over. I'm sure you've seen it, and I'm sure you've felt it.

You're probably thinking, but hang on, what if the person genuinely doesn't know the answer? Well there's always that, but in so many cases the contestant has an inkling or an intuition that they don't trust, or they simply don't allow themselves to relax and calm down to a point that really opens the mind. Consider that we take in approximately 11 million bits of information per second, and to compress this massive inbound information, we filter it to what we feel is relevant and not relevant to us. Just imagine how much useful, relevant and crucial information has been lost through the compression process that could have answered that million-dollar question, helped us pass that exam, say the right thing at that job interview, etc., because we simply deemed it as irrelevant. Well, that's because our RAS (Reticular Activating System) was so poorly tuned and we simply weren't looking or focusing on the right information to assist us with our own goals. Our RAS may have been set to 'gossip', 'negativity', 'manipulation', 'finding fault', 'triggering or feeding a belief about something' in what I call the *"See, I-told-you-gene"*.

I affectionately refer to it as the "See, I-told-you-gene" because people are more ready to accept a point if it comes with a bit of humour and recognition, which is essentially what comedy is; recognising behaviours and habits in ourselves. It's absolutely incredible how far people will go to sabotage their own success just to show you something can't be done. In that moment when they manage to prove their ego right, the brain awards the body with a dose of dopamine, so the process actually becomes addictive. You begin to feel good about being right, even though being right involves something unhelpful toward you. You can resonate with this hopefully? Coming back to what we can really do then to train ourselves toward success, well there's a lot, but it's going to involve a lot of re-training of faulty programming you've picked up over the years.

First things first, recognise how paradoxical comfort can be. The 'known' is a bigger driver than the unknown even if the 'known' is horrific or doesn't serve you. When you really think about it, that place called the 'known', whether it's a relationship, an area, a city, a restaurant, a level of income, a job, a company, a boss or whatever it is, it's a big pull. The ego rationalises it as, "Well it's not great, but it's familiar, so we'll just stick with it". There's so much more narrative behind that statement and it differs for each one of us, only you can really reflect on why the known is so powerful for you. It's one to think about.

When it comes to change, transformation, transcendence and fulfilment, there's a set process that I've learnt over the years from the fabulous personal development sources and shared with many others.

Step 1
We have to first have a goal, or a number of goals. Maybe one big goal, a goal so big it seems unachievable or unrealistic, and most

certainly to most people around you it will seem ridiculous and a bit naive of you to even be thinking about it. You'll know when you're there because you won't know how to actually achieve it, if you do know how to achieve the goal, it's nothing more than a task you haven't done yet.

Step 2

Once you've set your goal, you're going to have to write it down somewhere. By doing this, you're putting yourself in the minority of people immediately. Just think how many people are following a blueprint for life that is the exact same as their parents, and their parents before them, and their parents before … "Get a good job, work hard, save for retirement, etc." There's absolutely nothing wrong with that, but I've assumed you're reading this book because you are looking for more? Then stay with me.

Step 3

When you've written your goal down, you should start carrying it around with you. Keep it in a small plastic slip and keep it in good condition. At this stage you are now in the minority of the minority. Everybody leaves the house with their keys, their phone, and their wallet, but how many people pick up their goal card each day and have it on their person? I don't know the percentage but it's very few.

Step 4

Review your goal as many times as you can each day. Just as and when you remember, take it out and read it. You'll know what it says and it's not about going through a routine ritual of reading and hoping for the best. Anybody who thinks or perhaps interprets the theory of the Law of Attraction as just 'thinking about something and it happening' is seriously misguided. Yes, I've also seen and read the critics who strongly oppose the idea that focusing on something isn't going to manifest anything, and it's such a shame they've misinterpreted the theory in such a simplistic way. It's far, far deeper than this.

Reading the goal is a suggestive exercise. Suggestion to the brain is like a channel changer, it brings us back to the 'problem' or 'objective' that we have set for ourselves, and all that untapped potential in our subconscious mind as well as all that compressed information that we take in each and every day that sits even deeper in our unconscious mind, is activated and assists. Think of it like this: whatever it is you want in life, there is a person or persons on this planet that can directly help you get it, you just have to be open to going beyond the 'known' to reach out and connect with them. Reading your goal deeply and with meaning starts to lay down neural pathways, and begins to a create a kinaesthetic connection with suggestions, solutions, ideas and opportunities that start to come in from a re-tuned RAS (Reticular Activating System) – Remember this?

TO SUMMARIZE

You'll have a new batch of ideas, these ideas will transform into values and beliefs, which in turn will start to change the way you behave. You'll start doing the things that are important to your goal. All of a sudden, the old nonsense you used to focus on will disappear, the person that cuts you off on the road becomes irrelevant, the haters on social media just seem to dissipate, the naysayers wander off, and the more you stay focused on this goal of success, the more powerful your focus on the solutions become, and the more confidence you begin to invest in it. But you've got to take that first step. Just set those goals big, aim for the stars and I'm sure if you reach the moon you won't be disappointed. As the late great Jim Rohn said, "Work harder on yourself than you do on your job". As soon as you begin that process, it becomes a life-long obsession and the wonderful thing is the more you learn about yourself the more you'll learn about other people, because we are, after all, pretty much the same.

About Andy

Now in his 18th year on the front line of the personal training and commercial gym world, Andy McGlynn has been involved in some incredible transitions over that time which has given him an understanding and a level of experience which is second to none.

Backed up with his MBA (Masters in Business Administration), his Masters in Clinical Nutrition, and studies with the Poliquin Institute, CHEK Institute, National Academy of Sports Medicine and Association of Functional Diagnostic Nutrition, these all help to make Andy one of the most diversely and extensively-qualified and experienced Personal Trainers in the world.

As the CEO of GSquared Health Clubs, he also assists a small client base with optimal health and physical and mental performance through the use of lab-testing reports. He incorporates reports on Adrenal function, Gastro-Intestinal inflammation, Blood sugar regulation and Thyroid function and food intolerances, in order to provide a service that is unquestionably the highest standard in personal and private coaching.

As a speaker, presenter and writer, Andy has delivered live trainings to PT's, coaches, health care practitioners and the general public for well over 14 years, and has an ability to explain complex processes in a demystified and simplified way to help the audience raise their awareness of advanced, holistic matters that can have a profound and life-changing impact on their entire life.

Throughout his career, Andy McGlynn has repeatedly built and nationally-scaled multi-site personal training groups and has been instrumental in introducing successful PT cultures across many of the towns and cities within the UK. He was credited by earlier generations of fitness industry senior management figures as being 'fundamental' in creating the PT culture specifically within the City of Manchester in the early 00's.

The benefit of Andy's experience and knowledge of operating within commercial gyms and health club's filters through to GSquared Health Clubs, a project set to expand throughout the major cities of the UK, Europe and beyond, with the first location in the iconic St Anne's Square in Manchester, England.

Qualifications: MBA, MSc in Clinical Nutrition, BSc Sport & Exercise Science and Coaching, CHEK Exercise Coach, Holistic Lifestyle Coach 2, Poliquin Bio-Signature Modulation, Poliquin Instant Muscle Activation Techniques, NASM Performance Enhancement Specialist, NSCA Certified Strength Conditioning Specialist, Grey Cook 7 Point Functional Movement Screen, Poliquin Institute Optimal gut health for metabolic performance, Poliquin Institute Effects of stress on sleep.

Andy can be contacted through:
- www.gsquaredclubs.com
- enquiries@gsquaredclubs.com
- www.andymcglynn.com

CHAPTER 6

SEVEN SUCCESS SECRETS LEARNED AS AN ENTREPRENEUR
THAT NOBODY TOLD ME

BY JOEL LUCE

As I was looking at the rows of booths that lined the hallway of the crowded trade show, middle-aged, balding men telling crude jokes, and every other car in the parking lot a Ford Taurus, I was overwhelmed with the feeling of, "I don't want to be like that!" I had grander plans and ambitions than to be selling my entire career. I wanted to own my own business and make a difference in people's lives and my family's life.

I was transitioning from a job in early 1994 when I met a gentleman at a tradeshow, the same tradeshow with all those Taurus-driving-bald-headed-bad-joke-telling-salesmen, and we struck up a conversation. Immediately he asked if I would come to check out the company he worked for. I agreed to meet him on a Friday afternoon after playing golf that morning. He was the General Manager of a very large printing company, and I met with him and the President of the company, and they introduced me to the founder, an older Italian man named Nick. We walked into Nick's office, and I saw a putter in the corner of his office and asked, "Do you play golf?" he said. "Of course I do." I said, "Nick, guess what I did this morning? I hit a hole in one!" He answered in his gruff Italian-American voice, "I've been playing for 50 years, and I've never hit a hole-in-one!" I went on to tell him I hit a hole-in-one that morning on the 13th hole, and before I left his office, he told the General Manager and the President of the company to "Hire this Kid!" Little did Nick know that day that I would buy his company from him 13 years later and become the CEO.

That leads me to my first Success Secret. I say these are secrets because I didn't have anyone tell me how to do what I wanted to do. There are no Masters Degrees in creating a business within a business, raising ridiculous amounts of capital, transforming a 50-year-old company, and buying a $50 million business, at least not from any universities that I know.

Success Secret #1:
Never Discount Chance Meetings or Phone Calls

A chance meeting is like scratching a lotto ticket; you never know what you're going to get. If I had discounted or brushed off that guy at the tradeshow that day, I would have missed the most significant opportunity in my entire career. Always consider random meetings or acquaintances. Always ponder whether they can help you move closer to your goals and dreams. And always go by what your gut tells you when meeting someone. Generally, in my career, when I have listened to my heart, sought advice from people I trust, and took a period of time to think about a possible move or change, that may have seemed random at the time, it has always led me towards success.

Let me tell you another reason to consider seemingly inconsequential phone calls with great attention.

After having left work early one night at about 5 pm, I received a phone call on my Motorola flip phone from a gal that I occasionally did work for at my old company. She was one of those customers that you liked, but for whom you did very little work. She went on to tell me she was at a new company, so I asked, "What company?" and she replied, "DIRECTV." I said, "What's DIRECTV?" Little did I know that she had been there for almost a year and was moving up rapidly within the company and needed help with a large project. That one phone call led to tens of millions of dollars of work and millions of dollars of income. I still have that same client 25 years later and helped them grow from 300,000 customers to over 30 million, and I gained many more clients in the communications industry all because of that five-minute call on my flip phone.

Success Secret #2:
Do One Thing and Do It Well

When I have been asked by young entrepreneurs, what's the one piece of advice that I could give them, without hesitation, I always say, "Do one thing and do it well!" Doing one thing doesn't mean only to have one line of business, but it does mean to make sure that the first line is successful, and you have the proper systems and structure in place to support it so you execute flawlessly. If you add a brand-new line of business that is untested, people are untrained, and your systems can't support it, then hold off implementing it.

When I started with Nick, I brought an idea to his company to launch a fulfillment line of business to complement his printing operation. We developed the plan, tested it rigorously, brought on other talent to round out the operation, and launched in a separate 30,000 sq. ft. facility. It exploded with growth, and in 24 months we added a digital imaging and direct mail center and an additional 70,000 sq. ft., while leaving the traditional printing plant separate.

The business that I created within Nick's business is one of my companies today, but I would not have been successful with it if I would have tried to smash it together with the analog print business. Your best path is to stick to what you know, get incredibly good at it, and make it successful before you venture out into new territory, and do that one thing incredibly well!

Success Secret #3:
Buying Your First Company with Little to No Money

Anytime you decide to start your own business or buy someone else's business, you're going to need capital. The big questions are: where do I get it, and what's it going to cost me? Unless you have a rich uncle who really likes you, or you were born with money, the only way I know is to borrow it or have investors, or both.

My story is a little different than most. I set out to buy the $50 million company I helped grow with $1 million I saved. The first thing I did was learn as much as I could about investors, private equity, hedge funds, and debt lenders. Then I hired an investment banker to help me raise the funds. Even if you have a good amount to co-invest with a private equity firm, they're always going to have a majority share. The other path is to do a combination of debt and equity, with a bank or different lender like a hedge fund, and use private equity for a minority share. In my years of experience, private equity rarely takes a minority position when the principal buyer is only putting in a fraction of what they are.

I decided to do a fully leveraged buyout or LBO. An LBO is an all debt deal, meaning all the capital I raised, almost $21 million, was all debt and had principal and interest payments like your house. The catch is, is if you default in any way, that debt then converts to equity, and they own the business. This is a very risky way to purchase a company, but if you have the stomach for it and the cash flow from the business is good, then maybe like me, you will think it's perfect! Be prepared to refinance all or some of that debt over time, because most investors want out between 5 to

7 years. After eight years of investors and two other acquisitions, I was finally able to buy them out and own 100% of the business.

Success Secret #4:
Adapt Not Just to Survive but To Grow

When the communications business of our company began to shift more to online marketing and communications, we had to adapt to those changes. When I say adapt, I mean to literally transform what you're doing and how you're doing it. As the corporate communications business began to decline, we saw a portion of our business begin to see a spike in activity. Our healthcare business was healthy and growing, so we made a pivot away from corporate communications and built our business to almost 90% healthcare over a three-year period. That one move positioned us for phenomenal growth.

You can adapt and grow your business. Here are three things that I learned on my own that you can do.

1) Never stop looking for the next big opportunity. Most of the time, the next big thing is right in front of you. Consider other areas of your business or your client's business that you could complement, maybe like we did by adding fulfillment to printing.

2) Continually pursue new technologies to support your business growth or the development of your own technology to expand into new markets as we did with healthcare.

3) If possible, try to shift your business to products and services that your customers need, not want or are nice-to-haves. We adapted and really transformed our business by focusing on regulatory and compliance products and services that are mandated by the government, and shed areas that were nice-to-haves for our customers. These are great recession-proof products, especially if you're a risk-averse entrepreneur.

Success Secret #5:
Don't Stay in Survival Mode Too Long

There is a need sometimes to go into survival mode, especially where the economy and world is right now. There are times when it's absolutely necessary to go into survival mode to protect your business, protect your family, and to protect your own sanity. But if you stay in survival mode too long, guess what it does? It shuts down your creativity, it shuts down your motivation, and it shuts down your dedication.

It's during some of the most challenging and difficult times that transformation and innovation take place. Because that's when you begin to think about what can we do? And what's possible right now? If you think about it, some of the most amazing products were created during the most difficult times. Over half of the companies on the Fortune 500 list were created during a recession or bear market. Pinterest was created during the recession of 2008 and has over 300 million people on its platform every month. Just don't stay in survival mode too long, you have to begin to make a transition back to growth!

Success Secret #6:
Develop Influence with a Purpose

Your relationships are like currency, treat them with value. It's not a sign of weakness to need others, we were created not to go it alone, but through the power of needing others and creating partnerships, it will help move you toward success. They could be the door to your destiny, and you may never know it until you take a moment to realize that it's always through others, and with others, that could lead to something greater than what you could do on your own.

Influence is the door that allows you to access opportunities you would have never had without that relationship or position. Those opportunities can then lead you to purpose and fulfilling a need in someone else's life, which is worth so much more.

<u>Success Secret #7:</u>
Never Stop Living

In all the highs and lows of owning and running businesses, there is one simple thing I had to learn the hard way. No matter what happens, no matter what comes or what doesn't happen...*Never Stop Living!*

Never stop living means to enjoy this incredible gift of life even when the economy is down, the stress is unbearable, and even without money. Never stop playing with your kids and taking them to fun places, never stop falling in love with your spouse, and running away for the weekend or just for the day. Never stop saying how much you love one another and need each other. Never stop caring for those that are hurting and unable to defend themselves. Never stop believing there is a greater purpose I can fulfill, and never stop believing there is a loving God who cares more for you than you will ever know.

As the CEO of two successful companies, a 26-year marriage to a wonderful wife, four children, and three grandchildren, I am here to tell you it's all possible.

About Joel

Joel Luce has been in the business of helping people live better lives. With the loss of his mother due to colorectal cancer that could have been detected early, he has fulfilled a promise to reach as many people with lifesaving products and services to improve and save lives.

Joel is the co-creator of a patented product and process for at-home self-test kits. With over 10 million test kits distributed and thousands of lives saved, he has helped to empower people to take decisive action with their health. His work has focused on taking the uncertainty out of knowing whether or not an individual might have a serious health condition.

He has also been actively involved in supporting and saving children from trafficking and exploitation. Through his work with several non-profit organizations, including **Thrive Rescue International**, he has been instrumental in helping rescue and restore survivors of this global injustice.

Joel is the founder of two companies, Previon, a company that creates healthier communities by enabling early detection through at-home test kits and empowering people to participate in their care actively. He is also the founder of Bridgecom, a dynamic technology and communications company serving small to very large Fortune 500 companies with critical business communications.

Joel is an inspirational and motivational speaker in small group settings and regional conferences around the country. He brings a message of hope and purpose to very diverse audience groups.

You can connect with Joel at:
- www.twitter.com/joelluce
- joel.luce@previon.com
- joel.luce@bridgecomsolutions.com

CHAPTER 7

FINDING EUDAIMONIA: THE FIVE FORMS OF SUCCESS

BY JUSTIN WALLNER

Once upon a time, there was a man who wandered through the land enlightening all who would listen. As time went on and his teachings were proven wise, a group of students began wandering with him. The movement grew bigger over time, and his followers loved him more with each passing day. His students became teachers and attracted followings of their own.

He became known across the land and won the hearts of many people. In time, even great leaders began to follow him and share his teachings. But he wasn't loved by all. Some were so threatened by his power that they would stop at nothing to destroy him. To the dismay of his enemies who thought they could neutralize him with violent opposition, his message was so powerful that not even death could silence him. Through the movement he started, he only became more powerful with time, his legacy of enlightenment empowering the downtrodden and oppressed for ages. His name and message echoed far into the future, surviving to this day.

Can you guess who this great man was? I bet you can. You see, while many details differ widely from one historic hero to another, this is the basic life story of history's greatest men and women of character. History admires them for changing the world in powerful and positive ways, and for sacrificing their lives for the benefit of others. This is the archetype of massively influential historic leaders, continuing through history until the present day.

***

One such historic leader was Socrates from Ancient Greece. He traveled through the land, teaching through stories that stirred the imagination and challenged the status quo. Many of these stories were dutifully recorded by Plato, his faithful student and scribe. One of their works entitled *The Republic* survives to this day and is required reading for many classes in higher education. It contains the *Allegory of the Cave* which goes like this...

Once upon a time, there was a man sitting on a stone bench deep inside a cave with several other prisoners. There they sat, bound in chains and shackles, not going anywhere. They sat there all day, every day; bound in their restraints they stared at the wall, mesmerized by the shadows dancing across it. The dazzling spectacle put them in a state of trance, rendering them unable to think or look away.

Day after day after day, they sat there idle, frozen in their shackles and chains, staring in wonderment at the ever-changing kaleidoscope of shadows. The true origin of the shadows mattered not to them. They had no idea what was causing them and no desire to know. Then one day, the man began to stir, awakening from the trance. He could not stand the boredom any longer. Enough was enough. He was better than this. No more shadows. No more lies. No more status quo.

In an act of willpower, he forced himself to look away from the wall. He was tired of being held captive and staring at shadows. No more. His life mattered, and he was going to fight for it.

Give him freedom or give him death. He studied his shackles carefully. He wouldn't be going anywhere in these. But how could he possibly escape? For some strange reason, he didn't have a spare set of keys lying around. Suddenly, in a flash of insight, it dawned on him – the shackles were unlocked! All this time he was sitting there by choice!

In one swift motion, he threw off the shackles and stood to his feet. Adrenaline surged through his veins as he bolted around the corner, fully committed to his escape. Breathing heavily with his heart pounding in his chest, his eyes darted around the cave as he frantically assessed his surroundings, moving quietly, carefully, avoiding any guards that might be on duty. The other prisoners did not seem to notice or care, their gazes still glued to the wall.

What he saw next stopped him in his tracks. He couldn't believe his eyes. He saw many strange objects moving back and forth above the wall behind their bench. "That's it," he thought, "those objects are casting the shadows on the wall!" A chill rushed up his spine at a terrifying thought. "But what are those objects, and why are they moving back and forth?" In a surge of adrenaline, his heart pounded as he hurriedly ran past the wall undetected.

Then it happened – his heart skipped a beat when he saw them. Staring in wonder, he marveled in awe at the sight of strange people moving back and forth behind the wall, carrying those mysterious objects on their heads! Who were these people? How did they get there? What was that brilliant light shining forth behind the objects? Excitedly, he scurries further beyond the wall, towards the light that illuminates the cave. At long last, he arrives at the source of light – a gigantic roaring bonfire in the middle of the cave. For a moment, he stares at the flames, lost in the magnificent glow of a recently unimaginable light show.

After coming to his senses, he continues his journey beyond the warmth, comfort, and perceived safety of this magnificent fire. As he journeys further forward, he discovers another form of light filling the cave. The faint mysterious glow in the distance grows stronger as he approaches. Gradually, the glow morphs into a splendor of blinding light emanating from an opening in the wall of the cave, drawing him closer like a moth to the flame.

He reaches the opening, takes another step, and is completely engulfed in light. Overwhelmed with emotion, he stands still for a moment, unable to open his eyes amidst the brilliant glow. With great effort, he slowly begins to open his eyes, squinting in the light. He opens them a little wider and a little wider. His eyes start to adjust, and faint outlines of bright objects come into focus. A beaming smile appears on his face as he sees an oddly familiar sight; on the glowing ground below him are friendly shadows dancing in majestic harmony around him and giving definition to the blinding golden blur of the new dimension.

After staring at the shadows for a time, mesmerized by their gentle sway, he has a startling revelation. If the objects and fire in the cave were causing the shadows on that old rock wall, what on earth was causing these? He shakes free from his trance once again and begins to focus his gaze higher up. *Deja vu* was upon him when, just as he suspected, a mysterious object became visible. It was a large, beautiful, and robust tree, rich in the most magnificent array of colors and teeming with abundant life.

He soon realizes that there are many trees, as far as the eye can see. As he scans the horizon, he also sees deer, birds, and wildlife roaming among the leaves, rolling hills and snowcapped mountains. His eyes continue to focus as he desperately seeks the cause of these strange objects and wondrous sights. As he looks even higher, he learns that many of the things he thought he saw were mere reflections in a lake. At last, the world of the real comes into focus. At last, he sees the physical world for what it truly is.

He proceeds to move his gaze further upward. He sees the mountains, the clouds, and the sky in their beautiful true forms.

Though his eyes sting with intense pain, pain that only increases as he gazes ever higher, he becomes more and more enlightened. Finally, after his long and perilous journey from that old stone bench deep inside the cave, his journey has led him to a discovery of the Truth of all Truths. There, directly above him, impossibly far away and high above the very sky itself, shone the golden luminescent glory of The Sun.

***

What is Success, you ask? Well, Success is subjective to a degree in that each of us defines Success in our own way. We are all driven by different passions, motives, and beliefs. You will find dozens of different perspectives just within the pages of this book. To Socrates, as he proceeds to reveal in the *Allegory of the Cave*, Success is not just the pursuit of Truth that motivates a long journey through the cave of ignorance to eventual enlightenment and illumination. Far more important is the obligatory return back through the cave to the old stone bench to awaken others and rouse them from the mental darkness of ignorance, breaking them free from their trance and inspiring the worthy – his fellow traveling philosophers willing to risk it all on a journey to unknown reaches of the mind.

While there are many different definitions of Success, as one obsessed with the Truth since early childhood, I can identify with this definition from Socrates and Plato. I also find great value in Aristotle's definition of Success, or as he refers to it, Eudaimonia (a Greek word loosely translated as "Happiness"). According to Aristotle, who was himself an avid student of the great Plato and also the mentor of the world-famous Alexander the Great, we can measure our level of Happiness according to five criteria - Health, Wealth, Friendship, Knowledge and Virtue.

FIVE PILLARS OF SUCCESS

Pillar I – Find Your True North Star

Before sophisticated satellites and GPS technology were invented, sailors had little to guide their rickety wooden ships safely through the blistering heat of day and ominous dark of night across the harsh, unforgiving and seemingly endless oceans. Fortunately for those of us who now benefit from global trade and travel, the North Star has faithfully carried humanity through history to make our modern world possible. It has carried us onward from hundreds of lightyears away, far beyond our Sun.

Wondrous sights of a canopy of stars shone down on the sun-beaten sailors who risked it all for bold promises of untold riches and brighter days ahead. From the stellar glory of the True North Star, high in the Heavens above, shone the very meaning of their lives as they braved the great unknown of the vast and mighty seas. If you want to find Success and lasting fulfillment in the voyage of your life, you must find your True North Star. Find something worthy of a lifetime of effort, move beyond that warm inner bonfire of your comfort zone and get going.

Pillar II – Trust Your Inner Navigator

"That's great, Justin," you say. "You make it sound so simple, but just how am I supposed to do that?" That I cannot tell you. You must discover most of this yourself, just like everyone else. The good news is that there are many tools to help you along the way. Let us begin with a general map that will help us to chart our course across the Seas of Failure to Ultimate Success. In the Northern Hemisphere, the True North Star in the Heavens is easily found by locating the Big Dipper, tracing a line across the two outermost stars of its "bowl" and following the line to the outermost star on the "handle" of the Little Dipper. As you face this star, you are facing North. Simple enough. However, finding our own personal True North Star is not so simple.

We can find our North, East, South and West using the Japanese concept of *ikigai*, which loosely translates into English as "a reason for being". According to this model, we find our *ikigai*, our "Life Purpose," by discovering and aligning the four elements of What We Are Good At, What We Love Doing, What the World Needs and What We Can Be Paid For. One of my best takeaways from studying Psychology at Hawaii Pacific University is the Myers-Briggs Type Indicator (MBTI) personality assessment, a tool that helps you discover your *ikigai*. Fortunately for my clients and readers, a twelve-minute MBTI quiz is now available online. With this knowledge in hand, you will soon identify your Inner Navigator to guide you in your journey.

Pillar III – Command Your Ship

Rate yourself on a scale of 1 to 10 in each area of Eudaimonia (Health, Wealth, Friendship, Knowledge and Virtue). Add these numbers and divide by five for your average Eudaimonia Holistic Wealth Number. This method will help you identify imbalances in your life, providing valuable feedback about what you need to work on. With time and effort these numbers will increase. Next, set three specific goals in each area. Educate yourself and adopt the Success habits that will best help you achieve them. How do you learn these Success habits, you ask?

Pillar IV – Mind Your Crew

Mentorship is one of the most powerful Success keys and it begins with the books you read, the people you learn from and the Success habits you practice. A decade ago, my life changed when I watched *The Secret* in which Jack Canfield appeared and followed his advice to make a list of 101 Goals. I did this for income and material goals, life achievement goals and people I wanted to meet.

I've met many people on that list including my top three listed which were Jack Canfield, Sir Richard Branson and John C.

Maxwell. Another goal I listed was publishing a book. Never in my wildest dreams would I have imagined co-authoring *Success* with the legendary historic leader Jack Canfield himself, co-author of the *Chicken Soup for the Soul* books which sold over 500,000,000 copies, helping millions of people to succeed. Simply by reading this book, you may now leverage his knowledge and expertise along with mine and that of our fellow co-authors in order to achieve more Success.

I remember asking one of my mentors how a high school dropout like him was being lured out of retirement in his fifties with a $250,000 salary, working and living in Hawaii on the company dime while owning seven large homes. "Simple", he said. "I read *Think and Grow Rich* by Napoleon Hill. Every time I wanted more money, I read it again and applied it. I've read it twelve times and here I am." So, I read it. Years later, I was interviewed by the late legend Berny Dohrmann, whose father Alan Dohrmann mentored Napoleon Hill. I also read *Rich Dad, Poor Dad* by Robert Kiyosaki and Sharon Lechter and, years later, planned events in which she was our Keynote Speaker. This is called the Law of Attraction in action.

Pillar V – Improve Your Vessel

Eudaimonia is a lifelong pursuit of constant improvement. As we learn best from modeling, the best way to master any skill is to surround yourself with those who embody it. Follow successful mentors who are committed to constant growth. Always strive for Eudaimonia and you will surely achieve lifelong fulfillment and Success.

About Justin

Justin Wallner is a leader, author, and business consultant who empowers worthy entrepreneurs, organizations, and projects to achieve higher levels of Success.

At age 17, Mr. Wallner met with Senators on Capitol Hill and was awarded a Congressional Nomination to the United States Air Force Academy from Congresswoman Darlene Hooley, noting she was extremely impressed by his strong record of accomplishment and leadership ability. He was welcomed to the stage at Georgetown University by a retired Lieutenant Colonel, then Senior Aide to President George W. Bush and Mission Director of Air Force One. They led a research team that recommended security policies adding to the discussion of the Homeland Security Act of 2002. Mr. Wallner presented their findings to hundreds of leaders including Congresspeople and one of the President's Cabinet Members.

As Regional Vice President of Phi Theta Kappa Honor Society, a service organization with millions of members, he advised 25 College Deans and their student leaders in marketing, public relations and fundraising for events with American Cancer Society and others. He and his team were featured live in studio on ABC Channel 2 Morning News in 2003, and he was also interviewed by the Executive Director of Phi Theta Kappa in a live broadcast airing at Anaheim Hilton Hotel.

Mr. Wallner has served as a Marketing Director for World Financial Group, Chief Marketing Officer for Miss Asia USA, Publicist of Higher Xperience and Ascent Expo, and Vice President of World Film Institute and Family Film Awards. He has raised millions of dollars for his clients.

He helped Higher Xperience to plan business networking events in Beverly Hills with guest speakers including Make-A-Wish Foundation founder Frank Shankwitz and Napoleon Hill Foundation authors Sharon Lechter and Dr. Greg Reid, founder of Secret Knock. Other speakers were late legends Olympic Silver Medalist Steve Jennings, CITY Gala and Summit founder Ryan Long, and CEO Space founder Berny Dohrmann, who interviewed Mr. Wallner years prior in 2013.

As Vice President of World Film Institute and Family Film Awards, Mr. Wallner

Co-Produced the 21st Anniversary Family Film Awards Celebration Event in Beverly Hills with many Oscar, Emmy and Golden Globe Winners. He helped to revive World Film Institute 20 years after its collaboration with Dick Clark Productions for the Family Film Awards on CBS in 1996. The show was Executive Produced by late legend Dick Clark who joined fellow host Charlton Heston in awarding Bob Hope, Ron Howard, Tom Hanks, Sandra Bullock, Neve Campbell and many others.

As a Member of the CITY Gala & Summit Host Committee, he helped to facilitate charity events with celebrity guest speakers including Jack Canfield (Co-Author of *Chicken Soup for the Soul*), Astronaut Buzz Aldrin, Sir Richard Branson, John Paul DeJoria, Russell Simmons, John Travolta, Halle Berry, Ashton Kutcher, Tai Lopez and many others.

Mr. Wallner has several books and a financial education newsletter in progress. For updates and more information on how to grow your business, contact him on social media or his forthcoming website:
- http://www.JustinWallner.com

CHAPTER 8

TAP INTO THE M.A.G.I.C. OF BALANCE TO FIND YOUR CREATIVE FLOW

BY MARIA FORREST

Knowing what changes to make in my life is easy compared to making those changes happen. I asked my grandmother how I could move from knowing what to do in my head to doing it in my life. She said, "Life is magical, jump into it."

The acronym of MAGIC helps me remember the mindset and heart-centered principles of success, and I believe it will help you too:

M = Momentum
A = Attitude
G = Gratitude
I = Intuition
C = Compassion

Momentum

For me, momentum has to do with your thoughts, creating your reality to go forward. It's when things are going smoothly and quickly. I got a job, a new car, daycare for my child—all in five days. I was in fear, but I knew I had to do it all. I pushed through. The more you think about something, the more it may happen, so dwell on what you want. In other cases, you may talk to people, and they talk to others, and all are moving together in synchronicity, falling in place like dominoes with green light timing. The more people involved with an endeavor, the more momentum there is. Some faiths call it: 'where two or more are gathered.' You have more ideas, more thoughts toward what is right. Then, you see changes. I think of the Civil Rights Movement. That's when I think of momentum.

   ~ Kris Gibbs, Angel Whisperer

The best way to keep momentum is more about surrender than control. Not that I would know anything about being controlling or being out of balance! My coach suggests I put my hair in pigtails sometimes and play super-happy music. So here I am, dialing up the joy–and down the nervous tension–in pigtails.

Being persistent creates momentum. My 11-year project picked up speed when I wrote nearly every day. What matters is keeping up the momentum, whether all of your efforts are keepers or not. (I would also like to thank Jack Canfield and many others who advised, "Finish it.")

Figure out what motivates you. Usually, it is your biggest and deepest "why." I want my social impact project to uplift and inspire young children to use the gifts they came here to use. Yet, finding motivation for my daily routine chores is harder for me. It sounds backward, but my best accountability partner when organizing my office is reporting back to my adult daughter by an agreed-upon time–with a photo or video of my tidy space.

If you stop, start again. Repeat. That's how momentum builds. Accountability partners can mutually build momentum. One partner and I texted Y for Yes or N for No if we completed the daily commitment of meditation, exercise, or whatever. After a few weeks, the commitment was a habit.

If you want to succeed, first you must be willing to fail. Stephen King figures his mother knew he wanted to be an author after seeing a nail on his bedroom wall holding literary rejection slips. He found a huge nail when the stack of rejections grew. What a visual for momentum, attitude, and action!

Attitude

Check Your Ego at the door. The Ego can be a great success inhibitor. It can kill opportunities, and it can kill success.
~ Dwayne Johnson, The Rock

After eight years of working on a children's story, I voiced my frustration by saying to a friend that I wanted to throw the story away. I remember, with gratitude, the genuine look of concern on her face. Three years later, the book is complete! Good friends can help adjust your attitude.

Here's part of the reason why my 9-page story script took me 11 years to write. My lower ego was worried about hurting someone's feelings with a great line of tension in my manuscript, "We don't believe in that!" I finally decided I was worrying over nothing, and in the end, that line never made the final edition. Now I can only laugh about the fear that unnecessarily froze my pen.

I posted a letter to my ego on my motorhome bathroom mirror when I lived on the road solo for a year:

Dear Ego,
I have good news for you. You have the day off! I'll handle your responses, beliefs, thoughts, and focus. So have a miracle day!
Love ya always,
Highest Self

- No need to be offended
- Choose to be happy rather than be right (Value people over making others wrong, within reason.)

- Let go of your need to be superior
- Let go of never being enough
- Let go of bullying yourself
- Be kind to others as well as yourself

~ Adapted from Larry Crane's
The Abundance Course Workbook

I don't know if I have less ego-driven thoughts, but I am quicker to change negative thoughts to positive ones. Now I think, "I can do this. I got this." Be your own cheerleader.

To keep a good attitude, watch your words and thoughts. Brene Brown's YouTube videos of her TED Talks on shame and guilt are currently running over 84 million views collectively. Avoid less than positive words such as: should, ought to, and try. So go easy on yourself, like you would treat a newborn. Allow yourself a few human failings, so you don't make the rest of us look bad.

When I hear someone berate themselves, I remember a friend's reply when I was hard on myself: "Don't talk about my friend that way."

Gratitude

If there were a dial to measure our vibration, gratitude would dial us up to a higher vibe.

In my life, I've noticed that what I focus on grows. The following simple exercise is from a book, *The Magic*, by Rhonda Byrne. She also wrote *The Secret*. Here it is: Hold a shell or smooth stone in your hand. Think of all that happened that day that was special and pick one special thing. This exercise beautifully calls to mind many wonderful activities that happened to you that day. If you write down, date, and collect all those special things that happened all year, you can read them on New Year's Eve. When living solo in a motorhome, I read them whenever I felt my spirits needed a lift.

Intuition

Intuition may come from beyond the mind and heart. The title of my children's trilogy 'came through' my life coach. As well, the title of my short article about traveling in a motorhome for a year came from a random stranger. I never did learn her name. After hearing about the travel blog, she announced: "The title is Stop and Notice." I never thought of a better one.

Intuitive people do not read minds. Their sixth sense may allow them to notice little facial expressions to get an idea of what other people are feeling or thinking. They may be open to help from the universe, from the other side, or whatever you call those nudges. The struggle for me is to quiet my mind to allow listening rather than a chattering monkey mind. We all have different strengths and *viva la différence.*

I asked 26-year-old, non-speaking Darcy Reed what are the main keys to unlocking your success in life and your blog. She said, "I go into the silence and my brain is wired differently. My parents know how to support me. Also, I don't care about success and that helps considerably." Then I asked her how can I finish my trilogy as easily as your wise words fly from your fingers to your letterboard. For right-brained and left-brained balance, I put her answer into visual comic strip form.

She added, "Then just wait. It could come as a picture, a sound, words, or feelings."

The more I call on beings of a higher power, things flow better and my day is more full of grace. I'd like to share a personal story of how my sister on the other side has proved to me that she is helping, and perhaps she wants a little credit. Humor intended. I opened a new bank account and followed instructions to set my secure pin number. The banker said, "That should have worked, try again." This went on for a second round. Then a light-bulb went off, and I typed in my sister's birthday. It worked. That's close enough to prove to me that my sister is helping with projects for children.

Grounding tips keep intuitive folk like me with their feet on the ground:

- Be present and in-the-moment with your family, pets or nature
- Animals are very grounding and good role models of being in the now
- Walk outdoors (barefoot to feel the earth, when possible)
- Breathing exercises
- Rub your feet
- Eat root vegetables
- Privately, shake off tension like a dog
- Imagine stress sifting out of you like sand in an hourglass

Compassion

Family is where we first learn compassion and also love, forgiveness, and kindness for others and ourselves.

Many people fondly remember Fred Rogers' preschool television series, *Mister Rogers' Neighborhood*, which ran from 1968 to 2001. His acceptance speech for his Emmy Award follows: "Would you just take, along with me, ten seconds of silence to think of the people who helped you?"

He followed by saying, "How pleased they must be to know the difference you feel they've made."

I often name the individual family names seven generations back and sometimes wonder about the seven generations forward. It helps that my mother worked for years making ancestry books for each side of the family.

Compassion for the person in the mirror is just as important. I was so impressed with the effectiveness of Louise Hay's mirror therapy that I added it to a children's trilogy, and I am inventing a toy prototype with a mirror. Louise Hay inspired me to have my storyteller, Magpie, sing: "If I goof up in a big way, I look in the mirror and say, I love you anyway, anyhow, anywhere." Adults can show the way with being forgiving and kind to the person you are most stuck with, yourself!

Bonus Fairy Godmother Magic—Tips On Writing or Other Endeavors

Once writing becomes an active listening
instead of an active speech...
Writing becomes an act of revelation.
~ Julia Cameron, *The Right to Write*

1. **Watch *Shark Tank*** and keep both feet on the ground for sustainability.
2. **Stretch your comfort zone**. Famous inventor, Joy Mangano, had a movie made of her life starring Jennifer Lawrence, Bradley Cooper, and Robert De Niro. In her book titled *Joy*, she wrote, "I get out of my comfort zone even now."
3. **Make it fun**. A successful day has at least one belly laugh. Some healthy children laugh over 300 times/day, and their energy seems boundless!
4. **Self-care:** Sleep, nutrition, exercise, listen to relaxing music, play an instrument or sing. Find ways to take care of you.
5. **Draw or Doodle Sketch your Dreams/Goals:** This is the most successful thing I do but could do more often. It is a bit strange, but when I allow my hand the freedom to draw my

dreams and goals, it's uncanny how my intuition then has a "voice." One time I drew a mountain cabin even down to the stained glass window a few weeks before I found it in real life.

Practical Suggestions:

From my tax professional:
- Get a loan before you need it, while your credit to debt numbers are good.
- Treat your business like a business.
- Within reason, don't give away your business card or a bookmark or the like unless you have a solid contact person.

Consider forming a company with 3-bottom-lines:
- Profit
- People (community/global)
- Planet (green practices for the environment)

Have Faith in:
- Yourself
- Your abilities to make a difference
- The universe

Take it or leave it, but my biggest breakthroughs came when I opened myself to help from the other side.

Celebrating Our Successes

My coach told me that I need to celebrate my successes more and anchor them. Olympic stars often gesture a proud moment of victory. Some of my first celebrations were retail ones of a Fairy Godmother cape from Spain and local Thai take-out food.

Light-hearted and ceremony-type celebrations:
- Gaze at a lit candle.
- Enjoy an ice cream cone or favorite splurge.
- Be in nature.
- Dance or sing like no one is watching!

- Go to a beautiful lake, stream, or river.
- Bring nature indoors: plants, flowers, pine cones, gems, rocks.
- Be outside at sunrise or sunset— at the magical in-between times.

For an insight into meaningful celebrations, read *Sacred Ceremony* by Steven D. Farmer, Ph.D. I love the book's cover.

If I summed up this chapter in one word, it would easily be *"balance."* It is my greatest gift to have a variety of talents, but living a balanced life is where my biggest self-made problems arise. Balance may be an appropriate topic in any decade or generation. Balance in one's masculine and feminine energies, balance in work and play, and balance in alone time and time with others.

Life still has many surprises. A life coach kept suggesting that I request membership on the Facebook page: The Light of Autism. The founder of the group is the mother of Lucia, a non-speaking young soul. I asked Lucia for guidance in writing this chapter. I am beyond grateful for her words on tapping into creativity with balance.

Only when you connect with the light inside your heart, where your divine soul is, you will find the right words to write.
And your creativity will be easily manifested on paper.
Trust in yourself and in everything that comes through—never doubt. You have all the knowledge and power inside you to be successful! Sending to you my love and gratitude for your work with children like me and other energetically sensitive children.
We love you and your work.
Blessings,
~ Lucia (12-year-old, non-speaking, diagnosed Autistic)

Lucia successfully communicates through:
- Communication boards and iPads
- Beyond verbal: telepathy and intuition

Remember to follow your joy
as you tap into the magic of balance to find your creative flow!

About Maria

Maria Forrest earned a master's degree in Early Childhood Education while expecting twins and teaching hundreds of kindergarteners. An educator commented, "Maria's best credential is raising four happy, resourceful children." She admits to making her share of parenting mistakes.

She wrote her first book in grade school about orphan twin lambs that were bottle-fed. She contributes a lot of what her elder clients call being a self-starter to the wonderful life experience of growing up on a farm and ranch.

Maria studied Native American cultures and the spiritual energies that she feels live deep in the ground that we stand upon. Maria Forrest has written four books related to children – three books under a previous name, Marie McClendon, under Whole Human Beans Co.:

- *Where are the Children? In a TV World or in a Tree House?*
- *Alternatives to TV Handbook*
- *The Healthy Lunchbox*

A combined total of 5,000 copies of the first two books were purchased, mostly by Waldorf Schools. Waldorf Education originated around the time Montessori schools did.

A non-profit publisher sold over 80,000 copies of *The Healthy Lunchbox* that Maria co-authored and spearheaded. Maria interviewed on TV and the radio. She is inventing a toy based on mirror therapy/play that Louise Hay said was the most effective and efficient therapy for confidence and resilience, even if one of the bullies is yourself.

Accomplishments:
-- Certificate at the Denver Office of Economic Development for Sustainable Businesses with 3-bottom-lines: Profit, People, and Planet
-- Toastmasters – Awarded the best speech
-- Co-Chair Speaker Committee for Businesses Honoring Spirituality
-- Volunteer for Planning Committee for 2012 and 2013 Summit on Aging
-- Women's Circle in Denver for financial fitness and inner growth: founding member

Choosing a more international pen name, Maria Forrest, she says that Forrest Gump is her cousin, with a twinkle in her eye. On a recent birthday, Maria hang-glided with white knuckles near Golden in the Colorado Rockies, stretching her comfort zone and living a dream out loud!

In 2016/2017, Maria lived in a motorhome nick-named "Ladybug," enjoying the one-of-a-kind feel of each place, touching base in Florida, New York, Colorado, Montana, and Tucson. Her article on her travels, "Stop and Notice," is posted in her blog mentioned below.

Real success to Maria is living a balanced life of work, play, adventure, and making a difference. Maria established Ladybug Publishing House for a children's trilogy, *The Land of In-Between*. This story is coming through her to help young souls stand tall in their deepest gifts, even if they are short. A one-minute video plus voice-overs of this trilogy are on both of her websites below. To redeem herself for getting the first volume out slowly, she is determined to inspire young souls and the young at heart, including the neuro-diverse or those diagnosed autistic.

Ideas to spread the trilogy's positive social messages of inclusion and celebrating differences are welcome.

You can connect with Maria at:
- Website: MariaForrest.com
- Website: LadybugPublishingHouse.com
- Facebook: The Land of In-Between
- Instagram: Instagram.com/mariaforrest.author

CHAPTER 9

YOUR BOOK, MY MISSION

BY MARK GREDLER

I want to share with others the fact that they probably have a story inside that they want to share with others, and they can do so by writing and publishing a book. And for me to be able to encourage others, I need to describe what I have learned on my path to do just that.

I have two disclaimers: I'm sharing my experience on my path, but we all have unique paths – your mileage may vary. I don't propose everyone try to duplicate my path, and I know some recommended actions are not things I have actually done, even though they are model actions – so do as I say, not as I did. Also, some of my most important learning experiences came from mistakes I made.

I want to share the whole process: developing an idea, planning and outlining the book, writing the first draft, revising and editing into a final draft, getting a cover and back-cover blurb, and formatting and publishing. I also want to share what I see are some of the foundations to the project, things that are prerequisites to the actual writing and publishing. What I want to share with you here is what I believe is a part of all that, the most important of these foundations, is how we deal with haters.

Here are the three most prominent examples of haters on my path to becoming an author. The first has to do with a blog I established at Thanksgiving 2010, called Good, Better, Best Love. It was partially inspired by a medieval Spanish archpriest's book of poetry called, *The Book of Good Love*. The archpriest contrasted God's love with carnal love, but often in a rather off-color manner. My blog was faith-based, but in 2014, after posting weekly for four years, I set the blog aside because of criticism from some haters. Untouched for over six years, it is still visited by thousands.

Second, I had begun outlining a trilogy of novels about an American living in Spain as I prepared to attend my forty-first high school reunion. I had started a vision board to support my dream of publishing novels. At the time, I was pleased with the response to my blog, and I had published a magazine article in 2007. In preparation for my high school reunion, I ordered some business cards with the word, "Author," under my name, over a background photo of a friend's castle in Spain.

At the reunion, I handed out two of my new business cards. The first went to Bill, a successful lawyer. He looked at the card and asked if I had published a book. When I responded that I was working on my outline for a novel, he replied that usually someone does not call themselves an author until they have published a book. The second card I handed to Andy, a successful doctor, at the end of a conversation with him. I noticed, as he walked away, he gently set my card down and left it on an adjacent table. After returning home from the reunion, the first thing I did was order new cards, with only the photo of the castle and my name. No "Author."

I still had my vision, even if I was not going to promote it with my business cards. I continued to collect scenes as well as plan and outline my novel, and then I attended a writer's workshop in 2016. As part of embracing my vision, I had prepared a mock front and back cover of my novel and glued them to my copy of the book that would be the basis of the workshop. At the workshop, the leader and author of the book being studied was surprised at my treatment of his book, making it my vision book, and commented he had never seen anyone do that before. However, the criticism he provided when I presented several key scenes to the group, along with some comments on my lack of experience from another student, led me to set my project, and vision, aside for more than two years.

As you can see, when I discuss haters, I do not necessarily mean someone who literally hates me in the sense of having a strong emotion toward me that is the opposite of love. What I mean is someone who has prompted me to become discouraged. It could be a matter of simply not sharing my vision, being a naysayer, or even providing honest criticism. The effect is the same – for me to become discouraged. In fact, I am still friends with Andy and Bill. While living in Spain in 2019, Andy and his wife came to Madrid, and I took them places for wine and tapas, and on another night, was treated to a fantastic dinner. In 2020, during the pandemic, I had a long and pleasant phone conversation with Bill.

Two months prior to the 2016 writer's workshop, I had purchased and read Jack Canfield's book, *The Success Principles.* In addition to filling Jack's book with copious notes and highlights, on the last, blank, page inside the back cover, I had made lots of notes. These were notes on how I was applying some of Jack's success principles to the writing principles contained in the book of the leader of the upcoming writer's workshop. I had noted things I wanted on my vision board, things I wanted to do with my web page, as well as my plans to make a front and back cover for the workshop leader's book I was going to take with me to his conference.

What happened was that I made a choice, without a valid decision-making process, to let my feelings of discouragement along with my doubts and fears of failure squash my vision. This is the key – the issue lay with me, how I had reacted to what I feared most – what others think of me, or what they might think of me in the future. The leader of a 12-step program I am involved with is fond of acrostics. This led me to create an acrostic for my key word of haters: How Are The Excuses Reducing my Self-confidence? That was the problem – I was converting perceived discouragement from others into excuses to give up, to accept negative thoughts, which was a choice, a bad choice, I made.

But in 2018, I made a new choice, I decided to return to my project and apply some of the success principles that had resonated with me in 2016. For me, the key was the set of the first five of the twenty-four fundamentals of success: (1) Take 100% Responsibility for Your Life, (2) Be Clear Why You're Here, (3) Decide What You Want, (4) Believe It's Possible, and (5) Believe in Yourself.

I decided I was going to write my novel, and that I would do everything I could to make it the best I could. You may have heard it said: People may remember some of what you say, maybe more of what you do, but what they really remember is how you made them feel. What I wanted to accomplish was to write a novel that would transport the reader to 1980s Spain, and make them feel some of the same feelings I had hunting treasure with a metal detector when it was still legal to do so (which it no longer is).

Earlier, I had spent too much time studying, analyzing, planning, and organizing – all escape mechanisms from doing the real writing. Then I was paralyzed by fear of failure. Now it was time to take action, another key principle of success.

I knew I could do it, so I got coaching, and I attended a novel-plotting boot camp. I worked with four editors, two in-depth. But before I actually started the work with my first editor, I communicated with two other highly-regarded editors. They were both New York Times bestselling authors, and both had edited books that had also become New York Times bestsellers. In both cases, when I explained I had never before written a novel, and that I did not want to write a memoir but I did want to integrate a lot of personal experience into the novel, these editors both bowed out of consideration – based on their perceptions I might not be willing to follow their advice and guidance.

Then I talked to another editor, Bonnie, who had sold thousands of her own books, and was also a bestselling author. We connected immediately, and seemed to be on the same wavelength. What she said resonated with me, and she had an encouraging manner about her. However, after several conversations, a different editor I had reached out to earlier responded. This editor was also a New York Times bestselling author, but in addition, was very familiar with archeology – a major theme in my first novel. So, I had a conversation with Bonnie, and she agreed with my thoughts that I would be best suited to hire the editor familiar with archeology, which I did.

Yet after several revisions and having a final draft, I still did not feel confident that I had a novel that represented my best efforts, and I believed it could be improved further. So, I reached back out to Bonnie and hired her to go through my "finished" product with me. That was one of the best decisions I have ever made. Bonnie not only highlighted two big weaknesses of mine and how best to improve those in my novel, but she made a point of doing so in a teaching manner, always encouraging me. She was honest but not brutal or overly critical, as we worked together as a team to improve my novel. Between her honesty and frankness, and my openness and willingness to re-write and make changes, I was able to really believe her praise and compliments. My self-confidence grew by leaps and bounds, and when we finished, we both felt that I had a really good novel.

I am a firm believer in not only having gratitude, but in sharing it with others. And remember – what is important, what sticks, is how we make others feel. So, as I was watching some *America's Got Talent* clips on Facebook, there was a twelve-year-old girl that Simon Cowell stopped soon after she had begun her song. He did not like her background track but saw she was nervous and took her some water to drink. Then, at his request, she sang her song a cappella and nailed it, getting a standing ovation from both the audience and the judges, including Simon.

After watching that clip and identifying with the feelings of that twelve-year-old girl, I contacted Bonnie to share that story, and share that it represented exactly how she makes me feel in producing my first novel. I wanted to be sure that she knew I was grateful for not only her professional services, but for her friendship, and that she has really changed my life, for the better.

I have shared all of that with you because during this 2020 pandemic, I have expanded my vision. I still want to complete and publish all three novels of my trilogy. In addition, I want to share with others who think that they might have a story, a book inside them, that they, that you, can do it – and it won't take you thirty years to do it, either! I want to share what I have learned, both good decisions as well as mistakes – including resources that I have and have not found worthwhile or beneficial. Everyone's path is unique, and I don't believe there is anyone out there who could follow my path exactly. After all, your mileage can vary.

As I type this, I am looking at the desktop mirror at my side. At the top, I have placed these words: "This is the person 100% responsible for my success." And at the bottom I have placed these: "I am not a victim / I need to forgive myself and others."

You too must decide to be responsible, believe you can, and follow through.

ഔഔഔ — രരര

I would like to make one request of you. If what I have shared has helped you or encouraged you, please take the time to send me an email at: thanks@markgredler.com.

About Mark

Mark Gredler is an electronics engineer who worked for the Federal Aviation Administration for more than 33 years, 10 of those in a Civil Aviation Assistance Group in Madrid, Spain, where he helped improve the Spanish Air Traffic Control System. While living in Spain in the 1980s, when it was legal to use metal detectors to hunt treasure, Mark took up treasure hunting with his oldest son. At the age of five, that son found their first ancient coin from 150 BC.

Also, in the 1980s, Mark started making notes and outlines for a future novel based on his experiences in Spain. But it was a long, 30-year process to actually produce and publish his novel, the first of a trilogy about an American living in Spain. He started the formal outlining and structuring of the novel after retiring from the FAA.

Mark had to overcome discouragement from haters, as well as fear of failure, to actually get his novel down on paper. Key to accomplishing this was taking action on essential principles from Jack Canfield's book, *The Success Principles*. His breakthrough came when he connected with Bonnie Hearn Hill, a professional editor, his fourth, and the only one who was honest and direct, as well as encouraging. She was every bit as much of an encouragement as the naysayers had been discouraging. Mark's chapter in this book is a look at how to respond to HATERS – how to turn discouragement from naysayers into motivation to do your best, and to become successful. His goal in sharing this is to be "that somebody" for somebody else.

Mark has published articles for the *Celator* magazine and contributed to the book *Juan Ruiz, Arcipreste de Hita, y el Libro de Buen Amor, Congreso 2017*. He presented his paper in Spanish at this conference, and it was published in that book and in the online Cervantes Virtual Library. The paper is also available in English on his website with its English title, "Similarities Between the Libro de Buen Amor (The Book of Good Love) and Sexual Iconography In Romanesque Churches."

Learn more at Mysteries of Spain on Mark's website:
- markgredler.com

CHAPTER 10

HIGHER GROUND

BY SOPHIA EDWARDS-BENNETT, M.D., Ph.D., DABR

[Dedication: To the Author and Finisher of our Faith.]

The Transformative Power of the Big-C (Cancer) Re-Attitudes

I once climbed Blue Mountain in Jamaica with a group of friends. A grand idea at the time, mystical even, laced with florid thoughts of bonding with friends, sharing, and cheering. And, all that was true, but the hike was grueling, arduous and much longer than I envisioned, not infrequently plagued with thoughts of quitting, alternating with self-probing questions about the impetus for my initial commitment to this venture.

But the travail was all anesthetized upon our arrival at the summit; at the cool of 5:45 am, with fresh June air whisking gently across my face as I stood, in the ensuing moments, catatonic, gasping at the emerging stunning sunrise. I expanded the ambit of my circumferential gaze to the captivating panoramic view, and the incredible aerial landscape below.

I stood still, aware of every heartbeat, every breath, inhaling the sheer awe of it all.
The view from above, an unassailable canvas of creation's wonder.

And there it was, a new perspective, while standing on higher ground.

I submit that there is a parallel metaphorical correlate of life, that is, a higher ground, preceded by seemingly insurmountable obstacles, challenges that inevitably conjure thoughts of doubt, and deposit seeds of fear.

But with perquisite marination in time, it unleashes our innate tenacity, resilience, endurance and fortitude of the mind, providing the essential coordinates to navigate our route to 'higher ground.'

It is from that vantage, that one's perspective is ideally perched – to transcend the metaphysical gamut, gleaning a higher order of perception, of unchartered dimensions.

The question is:

How do we attain that higher dimension that liberates our minds? How do we gain enlightenment that lends copious insight, adorning us with wings of faith?

> *The answer is, quite complex, variegated with critique*
> *As our inner battles are both personal and unique*
>
> *Our revelations, synthesized by our innermost truths*
> *Are our very own customized stories*
> *Colored by our experiences, and primed by our roots*

PRELUDE

My Serum of Truth
A higher ground-I believe, is where success is found
Carving a path where tales of my destiny abound
Epiphanies gleaned from a coalescence of vicissitudinous waves
Revelations from the oxymorons of life
Lends itself to the first of a series of: Prose for Ponder

The meat of the matter:
Revelations from the oxymorons of our lives

It's not monolithic, but amorphous
It's not defined, but irregular and unpredictable
It's not ubiquitously applied but uniquely ascribed
But it is, including, but not limited to,
The amalgamation of experiential encounters,
the exhilarating and devastating
The soulful good and the indiscriminate evil
The inexplicable adversarial and the welcomed collegial
Our failures and fecundities
The terrains of tears and the fallacy of our fears
The veracity in our vulnerability and the nescience of our naivety
The hives of hypocrisy and the hailing of honesty
The truce of trust and the poise of peace
These collective experiences amassed
Our reflexive reactions, ensued by reflections upon,
and revelations thereof...
The analytic appraisals and granular interpretations
They infiltrate our inchoate beings, exquisitely and meticulously mold us
And inform our evolutionary transformation to becoming .....
Until we indeed ....become...the true and best version of ourselves.
That's the meat ....of the matter.... of our lives.

The Real Heroes: Chronicles of the Cancer Patient

Whenever I meet people in any setting, professional or otherwise
Questions prompt my disclosure that I'm an oncologist
To which a frequent reaction is—'that must be really tough!'
And while it is undeniably difficult, it is also indubitably rewarding.
But, my experience pales in comparison to the overwhelming, indescribable, adverse challenges faced by cancer patients.

I often espouse the statement that my patients are my teachers, heroes indeed, with an unremarkable display of courage and candor, an irrefutable truth to which we all magnanimously concede.

CHRONICLES OF THE CANCER PATIENT

Insight on Invasion
Through my lens, from their eyes

Imagine going about your normal daily lives
Interacting with family, friends, and the occasional stranger
Enacting responsibilities at work and home
Making plans for the future, as we all do; vacations, family
traditions, milestone events such as anniversaries and birthdays
and other recurring social events.

Then one day you notice, perchance, a hard area in the breast,
a lingering headache unlike your occasional tension headache,
lasting longer than usual; an uncharacteristic cough, or
inexplicable weight loss that you've craved for in the past, but at
this juncture is suspiciously effortless.

Your initial reaction is to bury these cryptic feelings of uncertainty,
the discomfort of uneasiness.
But the nagging feelings re-emerge, as the growing knot in your
stomach wound tighter by the second.
So finally, you cajole yourself to see your primary doctor.
Now, let's fast forward to the moment of truth.
After multiple probing tests have been performed,
Your doctor walks in the room, wearing a solemn face,
A tell-tale sign of bad news.

And, as you hear the word CANCER, the BIG-C

Time seems to stand still

As you 'subconsciously' dissociate from yourself
And you find yourself in the weird unchartered space of feeling
'outside of yourself'

You observe yourself from a distance, through blurred lenses,

Listening to the now seemingly distant voice of your doctor describing factoids,
And the myriad of recommended treatments you'll have to endure.

Prose for Ponder

You listen with pause
With wandering mind
Willing yourself to hear the details
Some bold and verbally <u>underlined</u>
While others are italicized
Another treatment, another phase, another odyssey in kind

Overwhelmed, I listen carefully, in this decorated room with ambient light,
Translation, another battle in this life to fight

And you ask yourself ….
Is this really happening to me?
This psychological spiraling can be devastating and paralyzing.

The reaction I've described above, is certainly within the realm of a normal human reaction.
Understandably so, as after all, facing one's mortality is one of life's greatest fears.
And even after successful treatment, cancer patients are perpetually plagued with the fear of recurrence.
This psychological aftermath can be debilitating, so much so that their sense of self, life, its value and purpose, is trapped in a somber cycle.

Perseveration and rumination becoming their *modus vivendi*: their way of life
As it consumes their thoughts.

Wishing it was just a nightmare, rising each morning to the rude awakening that it's not a dream, but in actuality, their reality.

Prose for Ponder

Lonely with my tears I lie
With not a morsel of energy left to cry
Restless and confused
But most of all, my life I'm scared to lose
A dream I hope from which I'll awake
Then perils I see, will disappear for my sanity's sake
But alas, I open my eyes and find familiar space
As the flicker of light sneaks through the curtains and shines on my face
It's true, it's happening and it's real
Cancer is the diagnosis, and there's no appeal

This psychologically-debilitating stampede is concerning; but even more disturbing is the fact that several studies have demonstrated that patients' psychological status impacts their actual quality of life.

Now, due to the heterogeneous nature of the methods used to address the psychological needs of cancer patients, metanalyses of these studies (grouping the results of multiple studies to generate a larger number of cases and thus more reliable results) have demonstrated varying outcomes.[1,2] However, the effect on patients' quality of life remains consistent.

But sadly, many patients do not seek psychological counsel, which is consequentially detrimental to their quality of life.

One might ask, why?

Why don't patients seek psychological counsel?
The most common reasons are the diagnoses, required treatment schedule, and management of side effects are overwhelming and time-consuming, thus precluding the procurement of psychological counsel; or reticence to seek counsel due to the stigma attached to the admission of the need for psychological

intervention; or the unwillingness to endorse the need for any help at all, fueled by the need to portray strength and independence.

When patients present to me, they expect treatment for cancer. And that I do, employing all the knowledge and experience in my armamentarium. This approach, albeit dutiful and commendable, does not guarantee access to the psychological landscape of my patients.

As an oncologist, I recognize that my patients are entrusting me with their most precious gift—their lives.

It is within this contextual construct that I believe that I am uniquely positioned to not only provide them with the best possible cancer treatment, but also play an integral role in reshaping their psychological frame of mind. I do so by invoking what I've coined, the **Big-C Re-Attitudes**: to enlighten and empower patients to cope with their diagnosis, treatment and beyond.

These **Re-Attitudes** include:

- **Re**appraisal of Life
- **Re**storation of Hope
- **Re**clamation of Identity
- **Re**affirmation of Self-Worth
- **Re**habilitation of the Mind
- **Re**ignition of Purpose
- **Re**quited Admiration

How is this invocation accomplished?

Just as cancer treatment needs to be tailored to the stage and other unique features of a patient's cancer, a customized approach must be ascribed to address each patient's psychological blueprint.

But to construct, I must first deconstruct, to expose the warfare in the mind, frequently expressed solely by inner screams and outward silence.

To do this effectively, it is imperative that I develop a solid relationship with my patients, to inspire trust and elicit vulnerability. I do this by employing a customized, multistep interactive process, commencing from the time of consultation, progressing through treatment and beyond, to follow-up after treatment.

It is during these encounters that I observe, listen, and ascertain information, from which I can then formulate a custom-made strategy for each patient, to effectively infuse **The Big-C Re-Attitudes**.

These *Big-C Re-attitudes* are borne out of the exploration of several important, probing questions. The probing questions are directed toward my patients and me.

Yes indeed, the formulation of the *Big-C Re-Attitudes* requires my equal participation. This reciprocity evokes vulnerability and endears trust.

What are these probing questions?

I'll highlight a few.....

1) What do you most treasure or enjoy about life?
2) What qualities do patients emanate; in other words, what unique attributes do I discern in my patients, that can be augmented and refocused toward their own psychological development?
3) What lessons does each patient teach those they encounter?
4) How have these lessons learned contributed to the enrichment of the lives of patients' family, friends, and other close encounters?

Information gleaned from these questions, yields a new narrative that I can utilize to inform and construct a customized set of **Big-C Re-Attitudes** for each patient.

So, in effect, I 'plant the seeds' to eventually harvest The Big-C Re-Attitudes.

These attributes, although closely intertwined, must be unearthed by the execution of a systematic, methodical, ardent and sequential process, with measured sedimentation and filtering, given the complex psychological state of a cancer patient.

However, the results yield a defined tool-set, designed to be applied in their daily lives, transforming their minds to create healthier psychological beings.

A truly remarkable dividend, is that upon the repetitive application of this algorithm, cancer patients are also uniquely positioned, having experienced its transmuting effects, to authentically disseminate the 'gospel' of the *Big-C Re-Attitudes*, by imparting their 'serum of truth'.

An even more auspicious prospect is, that upon propagation by, and to other, cancer patients, the baton can be relayed to friends and colleagues, whose lives have also been directly or indirectly affected by cancer, resulting in a ripple effect. Simply remarkable.

Prose for Ponder

Restoration of Hope

This battle of hope
Is riddled with uncertainty
It's the life unknown
The one we dare, while the failures we fear
The dreaded days we face
While anticipated ones we embrace
It's the joys we treasure
With all the struggles unmeasured
But with armors of love, swords of truth
Inner strength and minds astute
Giving up, we ebulliently refuse
We have but one life, and it's ours to lose,
So we're ready for battle, hence, victory we will choose

Prose for Ponder

Reclamation of Identity

It's not the 'you' that they think they see
It's not the person they believe they perceive
But it's the real core of you, that you know holds true
That echoes in the words you say, and reflects in the deeds you do

Prose for Ponder

Reaffirmation of Self-Worth
Rehabilitation of the Mind

In me, but not of me
It is the unwelcomed invader, I see
Threatening to cocoon the force I'm meant to be
But I will spout my manifold truth
After all, this is my story, to boot
So I will not stay silent
I refuse to be mute

Prose for ponder

Reappraisal of Life
Reignition of Purpose

'Tis from the arduous journey
That a litany of experiences unfold
Composing a story that is destined to be told
That grief not wasted is happiness consulted
Doubt abated is conviction unscathed

Loss endured is gain secured
Hope unaborted is faith consorted
And......
Adversity repealed is strength revealed

PRE-EPILOGUE

We all desire a cure, the panacea for cancer.
But in the meantime, we can all play a role in enriching cancer patients' lives.

Of course, there is always a resistant force to any positive endeavor But, if we remain persuaded, if we are tenacious, intentional, and vigilant in executing our vision, we can all be beacons of light, transcendent of policies and protocols, honoring only the propagation of the seeds of hope, health, and life.

I am eager to share this transformative algorithm, The **Big-C Re-Attitudes**, which, based on my clinical experience, will significantly impact the psychological frame of mind of cancer patients, improving their quality of life and transforming their lives.

I also strongly believe that the institution and practice of the **Big-C Re-Attitudes** will inevitably improve the cancer patient-doctor relationship.

EPILOGUE

Last, not least......
Our patients effusively express their appreciation to us
Which I usually graciously accept.
But forthwith I pose this question—an idiomatic citation:

DO YOU SEE WHAT I SEE?

The answer underscores our _Requited Admiration_ for our cancer patients:

> While we treat them, they enlighten us
> While we encourage them, they inspire us

While we advise them, they edify us
While we heal their bodies, they enrich our souls
Because their journey embodies the resilience of humanity
Epitomizes the essence of hope, and encapsulates the true meaning of life

Join me in sharing this transformative algorithm with the world
So that we can expand this vision of 'Saving lives while transforming minds'.

…And collectively aspire to **Higher Ground.**

"For with Him, all things are possible."

Appendix
Acronym for The Big-C Re-Attitudes

HIS LAMP

Hope Identity Self-Worth   Life Admiration Mind Purpose
"His word is a lamp unto our feet, and a light unto our paths."

References

1. Guarino A., Polini C., Forte G., Favieri F., Boncompagni I., and Casagrande, M. **The Effectiveness of Psychological Treatments in Women with Breast Cancer: A Systematic Review and Meta-Analysis**. J Clin Med. 2020 Jan; 9(1): 209.

2. Myrhaug H.T., Mbalilaki J.A., Lie N.K., Hansen T., and Nordvik J.E. **The effects of multidisciplinary psychosocial interventions on adult cancer patients: A systematic review and meta-analysis**. Disabil. Rehabil. 2018:1–9.

About Sophia

Sophia Edwards-Bennett, M.D., Ph.D., DABR is affectionately known to her patients as Dr. EB. Dr. EB is a Board-Certified Radiation Oncologist who gained her medical and oncology post-graduate education from Harvard's Cancer Therapeutics and Research Program, Memorial Sloan Kettering Cancer Center and Cornell Medical College.

She has been a practicing oncologist for over a decade, and is not only passionate about cancer patients' clinical care, but has excelled academically, authoring and co-authoring multiple peer-reviewed publications in the field of oncology, and as an invited speaker at numerous national and international conferences.

Dr. EB has also been donned with many awards and accolades, including Best in Medicine 2019-2020, Who's Who Professional of the Year, Lifetime Achievement Award, Top Doctor in Multiple States, Patient Choice Award, and Leading Physicians of the World, for her clinical contributions and prowess.

She is eager to share profound revelations, such as the **Big-C Re-Attitudes**, a novel approach which she strongly believes will tremendously enhance the culture of the cancer doctor-patient relationship, induce positive psychological and physical changes in patients' lives, and thus positively influence cancer patients' treatment outcomes.

She also avers that the propagation of such interventions such as the **Big-C RE-Attitudes**, will diffuse a pandemic of inspiration to patients, their families, caregivers, and physicians around the globe.

Dr. EB shares inspirational insights via blogs and podcast through her channel *REVOXYLIFE* (Revelations from the Oxymorons of LIFE), on *The Success Network TV*.

Contact information for Dr. EB:
- Website: MyDoctorEB.com
- Email: MyDoctorEB@gmail.com
  RevoxylifeWithDoctorEB@gmail.com

- Twitter: @MyDoctorEB
  @Revoxylife
- Instagram: @MyDoctorEB
  @Revoxylife
- Facebook: @RevoxylifeWithDoctorEB

CHAPTER 11

STAND IN YOUR PURPOSE

BY THERESA REED

Where there is no vision, the people perish.
~ Proverbs 29:18

We don't always know how much we can withstand. When faced with challenging circumstances, we often feel overwhelmed. Retrospectively, we learn how those experiences will define us: where we find strength, character, and even opportunities. Often in these very moments, you will find your God-given purpose. The question becomes, are you going to succumb to or overcome the challenges at hand?

I want to share my story about a challenge in my own life and how it defined purpose for me forever. By utilizing a seven-element process, I was able to stand in my purpose:

1. **The System (your belief system)**
2. **Unpacking the backpack**
3. **Boundaries**
4. **Overcoming adversity**
5. **Vision**
6. **Plan**
7. **Purpose**

I believe these key components are universal and can help anyone unlock their potential to do the same. To understand where we are, we must begin with where we came from, starting back in 1995.

We had one name picked out—a favorite boy's name, Jonathan, meaning "God's gift." We had prepared in every way. We took parenting classes, were financially secure, and read numerous books. We felt ready to be parents, and I looked forward to being a stay-at-home mom to raise our child. We anticipated a joyful and predictable family life.

After eight months of a healthy pregnancy, we were told the baby's presentation was breech, and a cesarean section was scheduled. No other concerns were noted. One week prior to the scheduled due date, our son Jonathan was born. He was presented to us in a bundle of blankets with the most precious face peering over them. He was crying, but he was so beautiful. We were finally parents, and pride swooned in our hearts.

In our joy, we were oblivious to the scurrying of medical staff. Later that morning, our pediatrician told us she was concerned for our son, as he appeared to be in pain and distress. The doctor was unsure of the cause and decided to transfer him to the local children's hospital for evaluation. There, a geneticist confirmed the diagnosis of a rare condition called *Osteogenesis Imperfecta* for our dear Jonathan.

Osteogenesis Imperfecta (or "OI"), is a genetic disorder of the Type 1 collagen, the protein of bone and connective tissue. People with OI have a faulty gene that instructs their bodies to make either too little, or poor-quality, Type 1 collagen. The result is bones that break easily.

Here we were, new parents, with a three-week-old child who had casts on both legs and his arm, attending our first OI conference. But I'm so grateful that we did. We met with educators, medical professionals, and families to gather information and understanding of OI. We learned of the national and state support organization, OIF. We received contacts for experienced OI surgeons out of state. All of these paved a way of involvement, enrichment, and support that has continued to be valuable to us, even today.

In those early days, I learned everything I could about OI. As a family, we prayed and had great opportunities presented to us that forever changed the path of what was possible for our family, and for our dear Jonathan. I could feel in those moments how God had set me on my path towards a purpose. You see, OI presented arduous challenges beyond the norm. There were many unexpected fractures, out of state surgeries for rodding of his long bones and back, the transition to wheelchair use, and the management of care and comfort as a constant part of daily life.

I recall one season when we were extremely challenged. We had planned a two-week family vacation out west. All of us were so excited. We planned to meet up with friends and visit Mount Rushmore, Yellowstone, and stay at the Old Faithful Inn. We couldn't wait to visit places none of us had ever been. A week before our departure, Jonathan's arm fractured (with OI, fractures can happen without a cause). We traveled out of state for surgery but still hoped our trip could happen.

Another six days later—the day before we were to leave for vacation—Jonathan's other arm fractured. Full of worry, we drove out of state for surgery, *again*, and Jonathan returned with casts on both arms. We weren't sure what was the right thing to do at first, but as a family, we agreed to try to make the trip. So, we left for a vacation anyway. As we drove west through each state, the feelings of overwhelm and sadness slowly lifted. We were able to take in and enjoy the grandeur and appreciate the scenery. We had an amazing time together and were so glad to have experienced such beauty together.

But with OI, things can be full of ups and downs. After we had returned home, Jonathan was still in his casts. While unpacking, our family dog was startled by a noise outside. He accidentally bumped into Jonathan. That minor episode resulted in fracturing his leg. Dismayed, we returned to the hospital for another surgery.

Jonathan often handled life better than the adults. We gained great strength from his delightful spirit, from his overall joy. It was contagious to hear his laughter. And he made us stronger and more compassionate when we sought to understand his outlook. Filled with levity and optimism, Jonathan helped us understand what it meant to be purposeful.

We made a choice as a family: we may have OI, but OI was not going to have us. That's not to say I didn't personally have times of procrastination, crying, even binging chocolate. I most certainly did. We all had to find our ways to cope, our personal ways to overcome obstacles. We learned to prevail and remain steadfast through challenging times.

One thing that always was there was our faith and resolve. Proverbs 3:5-6 says, "Trust in the Lord with all your heart, lean not on your own understanding, acknowledge him every way, and he will direct your path." We followed this very closely.

We also learned to balance the episodes of OI and make room for the treasured good times with family, friends. We made space to laugh and have fun and focused on ways to make memories together. We all wanted not just to endure, but to thrive, and living a vibrant, connected, and happy life was a purposeful choice.

I often refer to the many challenging times as character-building experiences. Pressure and adversity often shape who you want to be. The question is: are you going to stand in the challenges of your God-given purpose? Or succumb to it?

Here are the seven elements I followed that helped me step into and stand in my purpose. I believe if you follow them yourself, you can accomplish anything.

1. THE SYSTEM

If we step back and think about it, we operate in a "system." A belief system can be influenced by family, work, school, religion, peers, society, etc., and is specific to each of us based on those factors. The system can unknowingly affect how we perceive, process our thoughts, emotions, and actions (for good or for bad).

One example is that we were all born into a family system. Consider the holiday Thanksgiving. My wonderful extended family is Italian, so lasagna and turkey have always been served for the meal. I'd never thought about that until a guest joined us one year and pointed it out. "Lasagna for Thanksgiving?" Sometimes you can't see what you can't see. If we choose to stay in a particular system without questioning it, we may end up just repeating the cycle. To define your beliefs, and choose what kind of person you want to be, must happen – regardless of what "The System" says. When you stand in your beliefs, you stand in your purpose and can live truthfully and authentically.

2. UNPACK THE BACKPACK

When we notice dysfunction or detours on the road ahead, it may be important to unpack "the backpack" of our old beliefs and baggage. One example we endured was when the hardship of OI produced pity from others. Although I believe people meant well, the pity really wasn't love. Their pity didn't elevate us: it actually weighed us down.

Once I unpacked that emotionally, I found there was a higher virtue in this. We could persevere and prevail in the difficulties, and the higher calling allowed me to lead with acceptance, peace, and love.

3. BOUNDARIES

Boundaries define between me and you. They protect us. OI consistently challenged me to define my boundaries. For example, for every social event or family function, I would also have to make sure I retained the energy to support Jonathan and the unexpected fractures and OI-related issues. I learned to say no, a lot.

I was also determined to allow Jonathan to experience life to the fullest. We focused and defined boundaries as to what we could do. Swimming was a favorite and doable sport; soccer and football were obviously out. We set boundaries and adapted and modified activities to accommodate our needs.

4. OVERCOMING ADVERSITY

Advancing through adversity comes down to a choice and starts with a decision to do so. Sounds so simple, …right? In the midst of a heart-aching challenge, it digs deep to the core. For us, it was about protecting our child. Adversity and how you choose to respond to difficulties really determines who you are. At first, it can be overwhelming. However, if you choose to be strong, you can overcome most anything life throws at you.

5. VISION

Proverbs 29:18 says, "Where there is no vision, the people perish." Sometimes self-limiting beliefs can keep us from our purpose. When you stop the destructive self-talk and negative patterns, you can find yourself open to a world of possibilities and abundance. Think of positive visionary language like, "I can," "I am capable," "I am worthy,"— whatever speaks to you. Open your imagination and vision for goodness and purpose. Wayne Dyer said, "You'll see it when you believe it."

6. PLAN

Benjamin Franklin said. "If you fail to plan, you are planning to fail." It's a fine balance between living and enjoying the present while keeping one eye on the future. Planning is an important skill, but it doesn't have to be all agendas and to-do lists to be a plan. For our family, one thing we always made room for (and planned) was to take care and have fun! How important it is to enjoy life on your journey! Whether out of state surgery or frequent trips, we included pleasant diversions. We met up with family and friends who showered us with love and kindness. Plan to take care of yourself, so you can take care of others in turn.

7. PURPOSE

Upon his birth, I truly felt that Jonathan's birth was divinely orchestrated. I knew then without a doubt that my calling and purpose would be intrinsically tied to his life, survival, and happiness. What we would overcome and accomplish together! And what a privilege to be Jonathan's mom. My purpose gave me peace, clarity, and confirmation—may it do the same for you.

From that first day at the hospital to today, we have been blessed with many people who have been a part of our lives and our journey. A lot of those professionals and sometimes now friends want to hear how Jonathan is doing, and I couldn't be more proud to share stories about his life. During the last five years, he graduated from college and is now employed by the university. He continues to be an active member of the OI community and support groups and research protocols at the National Institutes of Health. An extra blessing, Jonathan recently married his long-time girlfriend. None of this was supposed to be possible, but he did it. *We* did it.

Jonathan's journey, and all of what we have learned, are incredible reminders to cherish what your life is, and find a way to persevere.

Whatever it is you are experiencing—heavy weight, unending pressure, surmounting obstacles—is here to present you with challenges, and with your own purposeful future. Don't quit or give up, but STAND and press on! Throughout hardships and change, you can and were made to withstand, to thrive.

You were meant to STAND IN YOUR PURPOSE.

About Theresa

Professionally, Theresa Reed has worked in the field of Occupational Therapy for more than 20 years.

On a personal level, she has had the unique experience and blessing to be a Mom to her son and only child. Together they have navigated the world of *Osteogenesis Imperfecta* (a genetic disorder resulting in bones that break easily) for the last 25 years. The very essence of her purpose and who she is.

Their journey presented challenges beyond the norm and arduous. With a source greater than themselves and determination that OI does not have them, success and blessings prevailed.

Together they met with educators, physicians, surgeons and traveled out of state for surgeries. They participated as well in research studies at The National Institute of Health for 25 years.

Proudly, over the last year, her son graduated from college and is now employed by the university – all of which was not deemed, or understood to be, possible.

Theresa is a lifetime member of the Osteogenesis Imperfecta Foundation OIF, a national support organization. It has been her privilege to volunteer for the OIF and has advocated on Capitol Hill with them. She has contributed to educational publications and participated in the advisory council for the OIF children's book. On a local level, Theresa has organized support group events for those affected by Osteogenesis Imperfecta and their families.

Theresa most recently has completed her Life Coach certification for Life Purpose Coaching. She has identified a seven-element process to "Stand in your purpose." She established this process to encourage others to step into and stand in their God-given purpose, to identify and overcome obstacles regardless of the circumstances, and to press on and live life to one's fullest potential on purpose.

Contact information:
- Life Purpose Coaching
- Email: standinyourpurpose@gmail.com

CHAPTER 12

DARE TO SUCCEED WITH STORYSELLING:
PUTTING YOUR STORY INTO ACTION!

BY JW DICKS & NICK NANTON

In the middle of 1999, the entrepreneur had just cashed out of one internet start-up and was thinking about what his next venture would be when a friend left a message asking him if he was interested in investing in an online business that would sell shoes. Even though the dotcom bubble was at its peak, he was inclined to delete the voicemail and move on. It sounded like, as he put it later, "the poster child of bad internet ideas."

But when he was confronted with the fact that footwear was a $40 billion-a-year business and that mail order sales already accounted for five percent of those sales, he rethought the offer and decided to make the investment after all.

The dotcom bubble popped big-time the very next year, but the shoe company was still standing. It brought in over a million in sales in 2000 and quadrupled that amount in 2001. The entrepreneur began to see that this could work and decided to become more involved as co-CEO. He began to develop both a vision and a goal for the company.

The goal? To achieve $1 billion in annual sales by the year 2010—and to make *Fortune* magazine's "100 Best Companies to Work For" List. The vision? They would no longer be a company that just sold shoes; they would be a company that provided the best possible customer service—that just happened to sell shoes.

They retrained their customer service agents out of any bad habits they may have picked up at other companies, such as keeping calls as short as possible to make as many sales as possible. Instead, agents were directed to give customers lengthy advice, even to the point of sending them to competitors' websites if they couldn't meet their needs. The company also put new hires through a four-week "customer loyalty" training program—and then, after that program was completed, they made those new hires an incredible offer.

The company would pay them $2,000 to *quit*.

Why? Well, if the new employee didn't really care about what company they worked at, they would take the money and run. However, if they responded to the company culture, if they felt like this was the place for them, they would stay and be dedicated to the company's vision.

Over 97 percent turned down the two grand.

By the year 2008, the entrepreneur met one of his goals two years early—the company hit $1 billion in annual sales. And the next year, he met part two of his goal, as the company made the Fortune list of the 100 best companies to work for.

Tony Hsieh, the entrepreneur, had built Zappos into an incredible inspiration to the business world with its unique customer service ethos. And in November 2009, Amazon bought the company for close to $1.2 billion total with the understanding that it would still operate independently with its vision left intact.

STORYSELLING'S UNIQUE POWER

StorySelling is when you create a narrative for yourself or your company that's designed to hit your customers where they live. Our agency is a complete believer in this branding strategy, because we've seen the awesome results it brings to our clients. When you put StorySelling into action in your day-to-day internal and external business activity, you really do "Dare to Succeed"— and this chapter will tell you how to do just that, using Tony Hsieh and Zappos as a prime example.

Nick interviewed Tony a couple of years ago, and we will be sharing excerpts of that talk throughout this chapter. This exchange perfectly captures the necessity for StorySelling:

Nick: *I've heard a quote from you about Zappos being a service company that just happens to sell shoes. Most people think, "If I'm a widget maker, I make widgets, and that's what I do."*

Tony: *Well, my advice for any business or entrepreneur is whatever you're doing, just think bigger. Take the railroads, for example, they were a great business at one point, and then cars came along, airplanes came along, and now they're not such a great business. They thought of themselves as being in the train business, but if they thought of themselves as being in the transportation business, then they would have been much better off. We thought, if we build the Zappos brand around the very best customer service, then we're not limiting ourselves to just shoes.*

Zappos' logline became, "We may sell shoes, but we're really about providing the most amazing customer service on the planet." Their narrative became, "We don't care what it costs us in extra employee costs, training, time and even sales, we are going to break the 'normal' business sales mold and do whatever it takes to meet our customers' needs." Or, in the words of Tony:

Tony: We actually take most of the money that we would've spent on paid marketing or paid advertising and put it into the customer experience. We really think of those as our marketing dollars and let our customers basically do the marketing for us through word of mouth and their loyalty.

Now, let's drill deeper into how they brought that story to life—and how you can do the same with yours.

THE INSIDE JOB

If you want your StorySelling to be as powerful as possible, you must work from "the inside out." If anyone else who represents your organization doesn't believe in your narrative, you may be talking the

talk, but you're definitely not walking the walk—and, sooner or later, your customers are going to know it. That means you have to hire people who fit into the culture you want to create—and properly train them in that culture. Here's more from Tony on that subject:

Tony: We actually do two sets of interviews for everyone we hire to work at our headquarters here in Las Vegas. The hiring manager and his/her team interview for the standard experience, technical ability and so on. But then our HR department does a separate set of interviews purely for a cultural fit. So we've actually passed on a lot of really smart, talented people.

Here are four big action steps to take in order to ensure you and your employees are creating the story you want to tell within your company:

Action Step #1: Clearly Articulate Your Core Values

This is the big one. Your core values should become the bedrock of your StorySelling. We help clients create and implement them in such a way that they become essential components of their narrative.

Of course, we're sure you've seen big corporations paste giant meaningless blocks of copy on their websites and call them core values, and we all immediately recognize that some copywriter has been hired to make up some nice-sounding words that actually have little to do with how they do business. Unfortunately, cynicism is the instant reaction to that kind of verbiage.

That's why it's crucial that you create core values that are *understandable, relatable and actionable.*

For example, below you'll find the 10 core values that Zappos promotes. You'll see the language is very natural and the messages are very clear:

1. Deliver WOW Through Service
2. Embrace and Drive Change
3. Create Fun and a Little Weirdness
4. Be Adventurous, Creative, and Open-Minded
5. Pursue Growth and Learning
6. Build Open and Honest Relationships With Communication
7. Build a Positive Team and Family Spirit
8. Do More With Less
9. Be Passionate and Determined
10. Be Humble

Consider this approach when breaking down your narrative into bullet points for those inside your operation to take on board (and for those outside your operation to read and admire).

Action Step #2: Make The Abstract Actionable

It's one thing to say "Deliver WOW Through Service"—it's another to make it happen. Whatever your core values happen to be, you need to put in place concrete methods to transform those values into real habitual business behavior, both by employees and yourself.

For example, here's how Tony made sure that customer service representatives had genuine interactions with customers.

Tony: Our approach is no scripts and not to measure efficiency in terms of the call times, which is how most call centers are run. Instead, we focus on the culture and make sure everyone in the company understands our long-term vision about building a Zappos brand to be about the very best customer service. They know the goal when a customer hangs up is for the customer to walk away thinking, "Wow, that was the best customer service I've ever had."

Action Step #3: Hold Everyone Accountable To Your Narrative (Most Of All, Yourself!)

As we noted, the usual statement of corporate values isn't taken seriously by employees or even management; it's usually more of a public relations ploy rather than any substantial initiative. When it comes to StorySelling, however, your narrative must be taken seriously by all concerned. There should be incentives for masterfully following through on that narrative—and consequences for violating it.

Action Step #4: Keep Your Narrative Alive Internally On An Ongoing Basis

You know the old saw about sharks: They have to keep moving forward or they die. Your StorySelling narrative is no different— which is why it's important to find ways to keep it a living, breathing animal through constant attention.

For instance, Zappos publishes a yearly "Culture Book" that runs up to 480 pages long and continues to reinvigorate their StorySelling. Here's Tony on this ingenious innovation:

Tony: It's a book we put out once a year. We ask all our employees to write a few paragraphs about what the Zappos culture means to them, and, except for typos, it's unedited. So you get to read both the good and bad. You know how on websites there are customer reviews? These are basically kind of like employee reviews of the company. And we give it to prospective job candidates and even customers, vendors and business partners, just so people can get a pretty good sense of what our culture is like.

The above four action steps create the kind of culture that supports your narrative, rather than subverts it. And that's to your benefit: The secret here is that StorySelling doesn't just grow your business on the customer side—it also strengthens it internally. If you implement it effectively, you'll find your employees will feel as if they're part of something bigger than just another business. In turn, they'll be more motivated to fulfill your narrative, they'll work together more efficiently, and you'll find yourself with a happier and more productive operation.

TAKING IT TO THE STREETS

If you have your internal StorySelling tactics in place, then it's time to deliver your narrative to the outside world in a unified and consistent way. Every time you interact with the public is in reality an opportunity to solidify your StorySelling and cement your logline with customers and clients.

Apple, of course, is a textbook example of how to make this happen. Through every aspect of its external operation—from their stores to their marketing to their actual products—the elements of coolness and innovation are on full display.

Obviously, you want all aspects of your business to work as well as possible, but you want to make doubly sure that you excel to the full extent of whatever aspect your StorySelling emphasizes.

Here are a few external areas where it's essential that your narrative takes center stage:

Your Marketing and Advertising

Make sure none of your marketing efforts contradicts your overall StorySelling strategy. An ad agency may have the most brilliant idea for a TV commercial in the world, but if that commercial directly conflicts with the storyline people have already accepted about you, you're in trouble: The public will reject the message and possibly even get angry at you.

For example, KFC actually tried a campaign in 2003 that advertised how *healthy* their food was. Nobody believed their claims and an *Advertising Age* writer called it "desperate and sleazy." The reason the fast-food chain finally pulled the ad? "Brand protection."[1]

Your Corporate Communications

How you interact with the public as a company is also vitally important to your StorySelling efforts. For example, if you're positioning yourself as a slightly secretive and mysterious organization in order to hype whatever your next new product or service is, you might want to limit any exposure to the absolute minimum. For example, the Segway, the motorized upright two-wheeled device for pedestrians, is frequently the butt of jokes these days; however, before it was released, its development was very top-secret—and, to facilitate some high-profile leaks that would create a lot of excited anticipation, it was only shown to such luminaries as Steve Jobs (who said it was "as big a deal as the internet") and billionaire John Doerr (who said it was more important than the internet!). The pre-release hype and mystery was so huge that the irreverent Comedy Central series *South Park* did a whole episode about it.

In contrast, Zappos, of course, took a completely different

---

1. Kate MacArthur, "KFC Pulls Controversial Health-Claim Chicken Ads," *Advertising Age*, November 18, 2003

approach to its corporate communications, based on its StorySelling narrative—by enthusiastically embracing transparency:

Tony: One of our core values is about being as open and honest and as transparent as possible. So we do that with our employees. We share lots of data with our vendors, and we have tours that come through every day. They spend a full day or sometimes two days with us, and they're listening on calls and see how we score them, or spend a few hours with our recruiting team and we share the actual interview questions we ask and so on.

Your Content

Another very effective way to convey your story is to create content that explains and promotes your StorySelling narrative; this content can come in the form of books, articles, blogs, videos, speaking engagements and one-on-one interviews. Content like this positions you as more of a thought leader rather than just another business person out for free publicity—and, just as important, your vision is seen as the innovative business strategy that it is rather than a marketing gimmick.

We are big believers in this concept—and we work hard to place our clients in such major media outlets as CNN, CNBC, FOX News, the major network affiliates (NBC, CBS, ABC and FOX), and in such national publications as *USA Today, Inc.* magazine, *Forbes, The New York Times* and others. These aren't ads we're talking about—this is substantive content that showcases these entrepreneurs and their visions. This exposure is, of course, important to increasing their visibility, but from a bottom-line profit point of view, it's more important as a demonstration to their current and potential customers of their prestige and recognition in the world at large.

The real takeaway we want you to have from this chapter is you should never look at StorySelling as a kind of coat you can just put on and take off when convenient; instead, it has to be seen as an integral part of both your internal and external business image. While some lapses in your StorySelling narrative are inevitable, they should be minimal and quickly corrected.

When you tell a story with integrity and consistency, the public believes in that story and in you. That's how you establish that all-important element of trust—and that's how you ultimately dare to succeed!

About JW

JW Dicks, Esq., is the CEO of DN Agency, an Inc. 5000 Multimedia Company that represents over 3,000 clients in 63 countries.

He is a *Wall Street Journal* Best-Selling Author® who has authored or co-authored over 47 books, a 7-time Emmy® Award-winning Executive Producer and a Broadway Show Producer.

JW is an Ansari XPRIZE Innovation Board member, Chairman of the Board of the National Retirement Council™, Chairman of the Board of the National Academy of Best-Selling Authors®, Board Member of the National Association of Experts, Writers and Speakers®, and a Board Member of the International Academy of Film Makers®.

He has been quoted on business and financial topics in national media such as *USA Today, The Wall Street Journal, Newsweek, Forbes, CNBC.com*, and *Fortune Magazine Small Business*.

JW has co-authored books with legends like Jack Canfield, Brian Tracy, Tom Hopkins, Dr. Nido Qubein, Steve Forbes, Richard Branson, Michael Gerber, Dr. Ivan Misner, and Dan Kennedy.

JW has appeared and interviewed on business television shows airing on ABC, NBC, CBS, and FOX affiliates around the country and co-produces and syndicates a line of franchised business television shows such as *Success Today, Wall Street Today, Hollywood Live*, and *Profiles of Success*.

JW and his wife of 47 years, Linda, have two daughters, and four granddaughters. He is a sixth-generation Floridian and splits his time between his home in Orlando and his beach house on Florida's west coast.

About Nick

An Emmy Award-Winning Director and Producer, Nick Nanton, Esq., produces media and branded content for top thought leaders and media personalities around the world.

Recognized as a leading expert on branding and storytelling, Nick has authored more than two dozen Best-Selling books (including *The Wall Street Journal* Best-Seller, *StorySelling*™) and produced and directed more than 50 documentaries, earning 15 Emmy Awards and 26 nominations. Nick speaks to audiences internationally on the topics of branding, entertainment, media, business and storytelling at major universities and events.

As the CEO of DNA Media, Nick oversees a portfolio of companies including: The Dicks + Nanton Agency (an international agency with more than 3,000 clients in 63 countries), Dicks + Nanton Productions, Ambitious.com and DNA Films. Nick is an award-winning director, producer and songwriter who has worked on everything from large scale events to television shows with the likes of Steve Forbes, Ivanka Trump, Sir Richard Branson, Larry King, Jack Nicklaus, Rudy Ruettiger (inspiration for the Hollywood Blockbuster, *RUDY*), Brian Tracy, Jack Canfield (*The Secret*, creator of the *Chicken Soup for the Soul*® Series), and many more.

Nick has been seen in *USA Today, The Wall Street Journal, Newsweek, BusinessWeek, Inc. Magazine, The New York Times, Entrepreneur*® *Magazine, Forbes* and *Fast Company*, and has appeared on ABC, NBC, CBS, and FOX television affiliates across the country, as well as on CNN, FOX News, CNBC, and MSNBC coast-to-coast.

Nick is a member of the Florida Bar, a member of The National Academy of Television Arts & Sciences (Home to the EMMYs), co-founder of The National Academy of Best-Selling Authors®, and serves on the Innovation Board of the XPRIZE Foundation, a non-profit organization dedicated to bringing about "radical breakthroughs for the benefit of humanity" through incentivized competition and best known for its Ansari XPRIZE—which incentivized the first private space flight and was the catalyst for Richard Branson's Virgin Galactic. He was a recipient of the Global Shield Humanitarian Award in Feb. 2019.

Nick also enjoys serving as an Elder at Orangewood Church, working with Young Life, Entrepreneurs International and rooting for the Florida Gators with his wife Kristina and their three children, Brock, Bowen and Addison.

Learn more at:
- www.NickNanton.com
- www.CelebrityBrandingAgency.com
- www.DNAmedia.com

CHAPTER 13

SUCCESS IS THE BEST REVENGE!

BY DR. TERI ROUSE

Frank Sinatra said, "Success is the best revenge." So, what is success? For a parent, success might be seeing their child off to college. For a child, it might be completing their homework, or being selected to be the captain on the sports team. But where does success really begin? What happens when we are aren't successful? But more importantly, what happens when we ARE successful? Do we even notice it?

I believe that success comes in small doses and that sometimes we don't recognize "success" as a success. We see it as luck or something that is owed to us. But when you stop and think about success, it is all about making choices, owning the consequences of those choices, and being flexible enough to keep moving forward. To borrow part of a quote, Calvin Coolidge once said, "Nothing in this world can take the place of persistence. Persistence and determination alone are omnipotent."

I had a successful childhood. We rode our bikes around the neighborhood until my dad sent out his whistle, or the street lights came on. We went to the park with our friends, and we sat on someone's front porch drinking Kool-Aid. Alongside our

Kool-Aid, we had a 'Ring Ding' or a 'Twinkie.' Those were the days.

I did the typical things. I went to school, played sports, had friends, and finally graduated from High School. SUCCESS!!! Next up...college. For the first time in my life, I was away from home! No one was telling me when to eat, sleep, shower, or study. Study, HAHAHAHA! Well, let's just say that my first semester at college was not academically successful. BUT there was success. I went away...I lived on campus...I made decisions (some not so good). I grew up. I made mistakes, and I survived the consequences. These set me up for what was to come next. Ultimately, I successfully completed my degree (in 4 years), moved back home, found my first "big girl job" as a teacher, and started the cycle of creating success all over again.

As often happens, I married my college sweetheart, and in a span of six years moved from home, found a job, moved again, had a beautiful little girl, moved again, didn't find a job, worked as a substitute teacher, finally found a job (as an insurance sales representative). Ultimately, we moved to the countryside where we built our little house on our little green acre. More successes than failures for sure. Then the universe shifted. I'm not going to go into the whole story, but let's just say that there was anger, fear, humiliation and isolation that was not by choice, but necessary to keep the peace. Not some of the best examples of choices for my daughter, but yet...there they were. This, too, while extremely challenging, set me up for the next round of successes.

I found the courage to leave the situation that I was in and start over again. Now, at 36, I finally found the strength to say, "No more. I am better than this. I have value, I am smart, I AM WORTHY of so much more." But I needed to keep in mind that now there was a little person who truly depended on me and that my decisions would directly affect her. We moved back to live with my folks. Some would say that moving back home with my parents was not truly a success, but you see it wasn't where we moved – it was the fact that I took action. I made a decision! I made the move towards being my own person. And I set the example for my daughter.

Once we were there, an opportunity came up to move into the house next door. Another cycle of success! We rented...well, didn't pay rent, but cleaned and maintained the house that belonged to a childhood friend. I didn't turn the heat up above 55° because I was terrified I wasn't going to be able to pay the heating bill, and my former husband would take Kristen away from me as he had threatened to do. So at night, we slept under piles of blankets. And we would go to my mom's house to watch TV and warm up. We ate store brand macaroni and cheese, PB &J, canned soup, and when mom asked...we went to her house for a real meal. Challenges? Yes.

Success? Yes!

Then I met Fred and we got married. We bought a house and created our own mini Brady Bunch. But with this union came challenges none of us anticipated. We assumed that everyone would have a clean slate. I was starting a new job, Matthew (Fred's son), a new school, and everyone in a new house and family situation. Unfortunately, Matthew's new beginning included detentions and suspensions from school. His infractions included smoking on the bus, skipping class, and stealing a scale from the chemistry lab, just to name a few. Arguments about homework and chores became a daily event. Kristen would come home from school and hide in her bedroom. We asked the school for help along the way, but the only thing they did was hand out more detentions and more and longer suspensions.

Besides the struggle with Matt's academics, we struggled socially because we were often not invited to places because of Matt's behavior. And we struggled emotionally because we were constantly fighting. We felt isolated and quite honestly, we were all exhausted. We were at a crossroads and we felt like there was no place for us to turn. Ultimately, Matt dropped out of school... three months before graduation. We were crushed. Our little family was falling apart. We felt that the system had failed him, but worst yet, we had failed in our newly-formed family.

But there was success after this. I decided to make it my mission to help other families so they would never experience the struggles and heartache we all felt. After watching Matthew struggle, and Kristen grow to be the strong and independent woman she became, I started to think about how I could help other parents help their children become strong and independent. I developed a program, "3 CRITICAL & Heartfelt Techniques" to reconnect and transform your child's troubling behaviors, to help parents help their children be the best they can be. Today, I am sharing but three quick tips to get you started. Please understand that there are many MORE than three, but you have to start somewhere, right?

Tip #1: Let your kids make decisions: Give them control of something

We all like to be in control...of something. As adults, we get to decide much of what we are in control of. Of course, we can't control everything, but we make choices/decisions all day long. At this point, we've had a lifetime to make choices and decisions...easy and difficult. Right? Think about that. Our lifetime to make choices and decisions. Some of you may be saying, "But when I was a kid, my parents made decisions for me and had control over EVERYTHING." However, you probably made some basic decisions like which food you liked and didn't like. Or to color in your coloring book rather than on the living room wall (good choice). In your teenage years you decided to study or NOT study for a test. Ultimately, you made life-changing decisions, to get married or not, to buy a house or not, to move across the country...or not.

Some of the decisions you made were better than others, I'm certain. If you made a "bad" choice or decision, you hopefully learned and didn't do it again. That is life's way of teaching you, hopefully, to make careful, solid, good choices and decisions. Did you "get good" at making decisions overnight? Of course not! So how did you get there? You made small decisions, and over time you built your decision-making muscles and didn't even know you were doing it.

Here are two questions for you...

(i) Why don't you give control over something to your child(ren)?

(ii) Why don't you let them make choices and decisions?

Probably because it's uncomfortable as a parent to feel like you're losing control, remember that making choices and decisions have a learning curve. The more choices or decisions you allow them to make, the better they will become at making life choices and decisions. Think on that. If you never give children the opportunity to decide what to wear, or choose what to eat, or decide what to do first, how are they going to make good choices later in life? They won't know how to do that! You are not giving them control over everything...you are giving them just enough control over something.

Tip # 2: Understanding and Accepting Consequences

Consequences = BAD!!!! That's probably the first thing you think of, right? Well. . . Wrong! A consequence is not bad or good. It just is. Simply put, a consequence is just the result/effect of something. For example, it's pouring rain. You go outside with your raincoat, you stay dry. You water the garden, plants grow. Those are consequences...look... they're good!

Sometimes you don't like the results of a decision you make. You stay out late, you wake up late the next morning and miss an important event. Those are "bad" consequences. Giving your child the power to decide what they want to wear to school or eat for breakfast are a great start to building decision-making muscles! Of course, having some guidelines is necessary. For example, the kids can't go to school wearing a Spider Man costume, but you can help them by suggesting they can wear outfit #1 or outfit #2. You can offer bacon and eggs or cereal for breakfast.

<< NEWSFLASH >> Once children make their choice...they have to stick with it...no going back! Don't be wishy-washy. Why? Because then the children will think that they can change up their minds at will. And making choices and decisions just doesn't work that way in the big, bad world. So when they make their choice...let it stand.

Remember to consider the following when helping children make decisions:

- What is the end result of the choice?
- Who is this going to affect?
- But most importantly, can you accept and live with that outcome?

Tip #3: Creating a Flexible Schedule

Consistency is ESSENTIAL for all children—babies to teens. Children typically thrive on predictability, yet a rigid or inflexible routine/schedule can be a source of unnecessary stress. Every day isn't the same, although sometimes it feels that way. (Remember Groundhog Day?) There are little things that make each day a little different. For example, one day you have a lunch meeting, another you are eating PB&J at your desk. When these things happen, we adapt.

Here is where FLEXIBLE scheduling comes in. Make two lists.

#1 The *MUST DO* list: These are the things that you have to get finished during the day: You must feed and let out the dog. You must take the kids to school. You must attend the meeting at work.

#2 The *WANT TO DO* list: These are the things that are not essential for the day, but you would like to do: Grab a cup of coffee, read a novel, play in the garden.

Now here is the thing, especially for your children, their day should be interspersed with *MUST DOs* and *WANT TO DOs*. Hmmm...How does this work? By giving your children... wait for it...**control** of some things, letting them work through the **consequence** of the choice/decision, and when they have completed what they *MUST DO*, they have the option to do their *WANT TO DO!*

Wow...Let's break it down:

"If you do _____, then you can do _____."

Keep in mind that I used this method when I was teaching children with some severe behavioral issues, and this was my way of getting the *MUST DOs* done, and giving the students control all at the same time.

<< NEWSFLASH >> Children shouldn't just pick something willy-nilly. THAT is a recipe for disaster. So, this is why you create the *WANT TO* list.

Modeling flexibility teaches kids to BE FLEXIBLE. Obviously, some children are more flexible than others (just like us adults!). Chances are, the more experiences a child has with a flexible schedule, the less stress or anxiety they will feel. And probably they will be more in control of their emotions and behaviors.

The ability to go with the flow, adapt to changes physically, emotionally and behaviorally is a lifelong skill-set that continues to evolve through adulthood.

Ultimately, as parents, we want our children to be independent, capable of making their own decisions. We all want them to be happy and successful. We all want to help our children to become academically successful, and create peace in your home. Through struggles and challenges, building skills like making decisions and being flexible, we can help them to become the best that they can be.

About Dr. Teri

Dr. Teri Rouse, more often called Dr. Teri by friends, family, students and clients, is a wife, mother, advocate, teacher, and mentor. She is a traveler, an author, and a storyteller. She is many things. BUT the most important thing, she is a woman who cares passionately for the wellbeing of children and their families. And she has made it her mission to help parents help their children be the best they can be.

Because of her classroom experiences and her personal experiences as a parent/step-parent of a child with behavioral issues, she has developed a system to help parents help their children be the best they can be: *3 CRITICAL & Heartfelt Techniques* to reconnect and transform your child's troubling behaviors so you can create peace in your home and actually enjoy spending time with your child again!

She also developed a unique program, *Braver Than YOU Believe: Fearless, Empowerment, Control and Success System.* This powerful system has shown people how to break from fear and take control of their lives, empowering them to move forward fearlessly with greater control and achieving their truest desires.

Dr. Teri is a multiple bestselling author. She is a member of the National Academy of Best Selling Authors and a Recipient of the QUILLY Award for *Cracking The Code to Success* that she co-authored with Brian Tracy and her husband, Dr. Fred Rouse. She authored *Julian's Gift*, a picture book that was inspired by her over 20 years in the educational field in Grades Pre-K to 8th, and *Braver Than I Believed*, her very personal journal of her solo travels through South Africa.

For over 21 years, she has been a classroom Special Education teacher, Behavioral Specialist, Early Interventionist, Autism Specialist, Applied Behavior Analyst, and Managing Director of KIDS Interventions & Direct Services. She has spent the last 17 years teaching teachers how to teach at Chestnut Hill College, Widener University, and Penn State. Dr. Teri earned a Doctorate in Special Education.

She travels the globe to give presentations at conferences for teachers, school administrators, organizations, and conventions such as the American Horticultural Therapy Association and the Division of International Special Education & Services. Dr. Teri is involved with the Division of International Special Education & Services, the Council for Exceptional Children (CEC), Light it Up Blue for Autism, Autism Speaks, Lily's Hope Foundation and Uthando, South Africa.

She has been featured on ABC, CBS, NBC, FOX News, *Miami Herald*, Bay Area-CA, Boston.com, and more.

For more information about Dr. Teri and her programs go to:
- http://drterirouse.com
- Facebook: Dr. Teri Rouse
- Instagram: dr_teri_rouse

CHAPTER 14

FROM THINKING TO TRANSFORMING

BY CARISA FINDLEY

I have a very special bench. This secluded, public bench is unassuming. It's hidden at the end of a residential street in South Florida. The teal paint is chipping from age. It sits under a large tree with gorgeous views of the intracoastal waterway. Even on hot, humid Florida days, the shade and slight breeze off the water keeps it cool. It's peaceful, quiet.

I laugh thinking about the number of people who have sat at that bench unknowing of the magical powers it holds. It's on that bench, at the end of my block, that I dreamed up the most incredible vision for my life. I've sat there for hours, in the heat, caught in midday thunderstorms, all while picturing my future. It's at that place that I have visualized the type of professional success I'd have, how I'd serve others, the place I'd live, how my romantic life would look, and even the type of car I'd drive. To most people in my neighborhood, that rarely used bench was just a stop off as they briefly took in the view or sought refuge from the sweltering sun. For me, it was the starting point for some of the greatest accomplishments of my life.

Did my life need a complete transformation? Absolutely not.

(I mean, the scenic intracoastal was at the end of my block!) Yes, I may hate the heat, but I had a really great job with a wonderful circle of friends. I already had a lot to be grateful for, but I was getting an itch for something more. Maybe you know what I mean? Yeah, it'd be nice to live in a great home and have a nicer car, but this wasn't the itch. It was a whisper from a gentle wind, telling me to find my purpose. Then, a stronger nudge came telling me to shine my light. Finally, it was a giant push to get myself to that bench and figure out how I could serve more people.

If you are ready for a bigger, bolder life, one that you know is destined for you, the "magical" powers of my bench are available to you at anytime, anywhere. You, too, can use the power of visualization to bring your wildest dreams into reality.

Create the highest, grandest vision possible for your life,
because you become what you believe.
~ Oprah Winfrey

Visualization is the practice of using your imagination to see the outcomes you desire. Using your mind, you can create mental pictures of the world you wish to see, whether that is the view from your new beach house when you wake up each day, the sale of your business for more than you expected, a dream vacation with your family, or the way your employees rise to exceed this month's production goals. Your mind is a powerful force. The thoughts created from your mind hold the power to determine your destiny.

Here's something that select high-achievers understand—the thoughts you create and the visions of your life that you hold in your mind ultimately determine the course of your life. If you consciously use your mind to create uplifting, inspiring thoughts, then those thoughts influence your actions.

Imagine you need to hire a new employee, but you find yourself thinking that the effort to do so is hopeless. The level of talent that is available will never meet your expectations and you've only had disappointment before. How will those thoughts impact your actions during the hiring process? You'll likely scan through resumés reluctantly, noticing only the negatives. Guess what's likely to happen?

Now, try a different approach. Picture your ideal candidate and see yourself reviewing an abundance of highly-qualified resumés and feeling excited about how this next new hire will help grow your business. Do you think you will approach the resumés differently? Will you focus more on the possibilities rather than the negatives you noticed before?

The quality of your life is ultimately a reflection of the thoughts you've had. Good or bad, you've taken past actions based on your thoughts, which have placed you in the exact spot you are in now. Ask yourself, "Am I where I want to be?" Do you have more to achieve? Are you able to give in the way you want? Luckily, you have access to the tool of visualization that can help you reach the life you desire.

> *You'll see it when you believe it.*
> ~ Wayne Dyer

Science has begun to lift the veil on the power of visualization. This practice is no longer perceived as mystical or spiritual and it's way more than "imagination" or "positive thinking." This is the power of the brain bringing your thoughts to life!

We've had an idea previously about how the mind can transform a thought into a physical response. Just thinking about a lemon being squeezed in your mouth can instantly make you salivate, right? Studies show that when you give your mind the vision of a goal you'd like to achieve, the brain seeks to make that goal come to life.

- When we repeat behaviors, either mentally or physically, the neural pathways in the brain strengthen. If every time you walk into the kitchen, you grab a snack in the pantry, then the more you repeat that behavior the stronger the brain associates walking into the kitchen with eating. This may not be a behavior that benefits you long-term! Luckily, the brain is adaptive and new behaviors can be formed. Neuroplasticity, or the brain's ability to form new neural pathways, can help you break old habits and establish more successful behaviors.

- When the brain encounters the same event repeatedly, it looks for efficient ways to execute that task. It starts to seek out solutions so it can be attuned to opportunities that help to accomplish that task. Your Reticular Activating System (or RAS) is a network of nerves in your brainstem that acts as a filter, noticing and selecting information based on the beliefs you hold. When you hold a powerful belief like, "my business is thriving and our profitability is growing," your RAS will funnel information, ideas, and opportunities based on that belief.

- We also know that practice makes perfect, right? Visualization makes the unfamiliar, familiar to your brain. When encountering the unfamiliar, your fight-or-flight stress response kicks in. Your heart rate increases and your breath becomes short. That's not exactly the state you want to be in when giving a speech to the new team you are supervising. If you've visualized giving that speech flawlessly over and over again, when it's time for the real thing, you're in a state of ease, you're confident, you're energetic and focused.

You are the mental architect of your own destiny.
~ Bob Proctor

BEGINNING A VISUALIZATION PRACTICE

I started using visualization on that bench in sunny Florida to help me take my life to the next level. It was a powerful practice that helped me capture my itch of wanting more. If you too are getting that calling, you can begin with a visualization practice called "My Perfect Day." Whether you have practiced visualization before or you are trying it out for the first time, I've found this to be incredibly powerful in discovering what the next level of your life can be.

MY PERFECT DAY VISUALIZATION

Step 1: Find a comfortable place to sit where you are relaxed enough to let your imagination roam (like my teal bench in Florida or near a peaceful pond or in a park—a place that inspires you). Perhaps you'd like to listen to soft music. Be sure to have a notebook and pen nearby.

Step 2: Think about your perfect day from the moment you wake up until the time you go to sleep. When you open your eyes in the morning, what do you see? Where are you living? Who are you with? Move through your day doing only the activities that you absolutely love. Do you go for a hike or a swim in your pool? Think about the ways you spend your time working or helping others. Are you a successful CEO? Do you volunteer teaching theater classes to kids? Really dig into the details of your day. What does your house look like and what is the view from your home? What is the expression on your children's faces when you see them first thing in the morning? Go through your entire day outlining everything that would make it a perfect day.

Step 3: After you've envisioned your perfect day, begin to free write how your day looked. Write down the things you did, the people you were with, and the successes you've had in your career. Write down all the details of your perfect day.

Step 4: The next two steps are incredibly important. First, re-read your writing and honestly assess where you are playing small. This is your chance to get exactly what you want! Did you play within reason and settle for what you think is realistic? Don't hold back! When you imagine looking at your bank account balance, how much money was in there? Do you need to add a lot more zeros? You are capable of things greater than you currently think are achievable. That's what this practice is about. Edit and rewrite the areas where you know you can dream bigger.

Step 5: Now, re-read your perfect day and experience it with all the incredible emotions you'd experience throughout the day. This is the secret to amplifying your results from visualization. You probably already noticed that writing and reading your perfect day brings about a sense of excitement and pleasure. The more emotion sensed by the brain, the stronger the neural pathway becomes.

Use this visualization practice daily. Sit quietly and walk through your perfect day. Feel the feelings of love you have for your partner as you open your eyes first thing in the morning. Feel the overwhelming sense of gratitude when you hear your business partner express how much you've helped grow your business. Experience the peace you feel at the end of the day when you look at your loved ones and connect to how you helped make the world a better place.

ANYTIME VISUALIZATION PRACTICE

Whether you have an upcoming sales pitch with a large prospective client, a looming one-on-one with a struggling employee, or even an upcoming first date, the same practice from above can help you show up as your best self.

Leading up to the event, take time to visualize what a perfect outcome would look like. Before a training event, I visualize myself speaking clearly and passionately. I see the looks of smiles and nodding heads from the attendees. I see the training ending with expressions of gratitude from the attendees and I feel joyful knowing that my training helped improve their lives.

The thoughts I think today are creating the reality I will experience in the future.
~ Jack Canfield

From my bench in Florida, I pictured myself living in the mountains, sharing a home with my partner, having a career that allowed me to train and motivate people. I'd see myself driving home in my Volvo SUV with a view of the mountains as I was coming home to see my love. I pictured being filled with gratitude and joy. I'd replay these images over and over feeling a sense of certainty that this life is destined for me.

A few years later, I was sitting in a meditation and I was suddenly hit with a revelation! I opened my eyes and realized *I had done it!* When I looked up, I saw the mountains from my home in Colorado. I could hear my partner getting ready for work. I had a career that I loved where I could train and help others. I had even driven my Volvo SUV that day. That moment—that sudden revelation of *I did it*—is the moment I want you to experience! When you realize that the dreams you had for yourself are now your reality. That moment is when you realize your ultimate power.

About Carisa

Carisa Findley is a transformational trainer and international speaker that brings a new perspective to improving performance and professional results. As a certified mindfulness teacher, Carisa helps entrepreneurs and companies increase their business results through tangible self-development actions.

Carisa has spent over a decade in franchising, helping entrepreneurs grow their businesses. But her experience with franchise owners actually started at age three. That's when Carisa and her family moved to Florida so her parents could run their own franchise business.

During her career, Carisa has supported business owners and an array of employees through roles as a business coach, operations specialist, franchise speaker and as an adult learning expert.

Carisa is a native Texan and a graduate of Baylor University. She's been a featured podcast guest, industry panelist and hosted trainings in several countries. She's even lived and worked in Australia and New Zealand. Carisa's energetic presence comes from her passion for early mornings and fitness. She has even taught group exercise classes for years. Carisa loves blending her background in business development with fitness, meditation, mindfulness and adult learning to help people show up as their best self.

You can connect with Carisa at:
- bookings@carisafindley.com
- https://carisafindley.com
- https://www.instagram.com/carisafindley/

CHAPTER 15

FIND YOUR ACRES OF DIAMONDS

BY FELIPE BARGANIER

They say diamonds are a girl's best friend. Well, it was never about being the best friend; it's about the value they hold. Their value remains the same for everyone, despite what their gender is. If you look at a diamond closely, it's nothing but a stone. What makes the difference is that it's rare, beautiful, and one of the most admired gemstones on earth.

Only a few diamonds can survive the challenging journey from the pits of the earth to reach its surface. Moreover, out of all the diamonds that are being mined today, only 50% are believed to have the requisite standard to be sold in the market as a gem. That's why they are scarce, valued, and sold at a high price.

Now that you know the value of diamonds, I need you to think of them as a symbol of success. Why? Success doesn't come easy either, and it sure is rare! Who, in your eyes, is the most successful person on this planet? I am sure a name popped up in your head, maybe Bill Gates, or perhaps Mark Zuckerberg, but that isn't even the question. The real question is if there is anyone else that you can think of in their comparison? Barely a few names! That's how rare success is.

Anyway, I am Felipe Barganier, and I am here to engrave in you that success is as rare and precious as diamonds. However, you will have to dig deep within yourself to find your acres of diamonds. One finds success through blood and sweat, but when they finally do, they know that it is far more valuable than a diamond. So, if you are someone looking for tips and tricks to find your acres of diamonds, you are at the right place and moving in the right direction.

THE MOST IMPORTANT TIP: LOOK FOR IT IN THE MOST UNEXPECTED PLACES

Success comes to you when you are least expecting it. It comes to you in places you never even imagined you would find it. If I talk about myself, yes, I did find my diamonds, if not acres of them. And yes, they were in the places that I least expected them to be. So, here's my journey to success for people looking for inspiration.

The greatest or most significant wins that I received in my business have always been in less desirable places. I often found success in a place where most people would never look for it. Sometimes, abandoned buildings hide the most precious stones, value them. I need you to be always mindful that your business may not flourish in the way you thought it would, or in the areas you thought it is going to be. Still, the crucial part is that it should be successful. You will find that success underneath many layers and in the most unexpected corners. The only condition is to keep digging!

When I started my business back in 2001, my first client, who was also my biggest client for that period, lived at a considerable distance from me. I had to drive an hour and a half away to secure that client. Yet, it was actually done when the individual called for my services. The opportunity at that time seemed small because I was supposed to deal with only a one-off situation for one person. However, it ended up morphing into servicing her entire employee group of about 13,000 employees for 15 years, which was incredibly lucrative for me.

This is a fantastic example that teaches us never to take any opportunity for granted. Never look at something as if it's never going to give you the profits you expect. Treat every client and every opportunity with equal enthusiasm. Who knows if one of them is hiding beneath the diamonds you are looking for?

TAKE EVERY OPPORTUNITY SERIOUSLY

Here's another story from which you may take inspiration. It will help you learn that an opportunity only knocks once at your door. If you do not open the door at the right time, it might leave before you know it. When I first left corporate America in 2001, it was also the year when my ex-wife's aunt passed away.

She was married to a prominent figure on the radio in Atlanta. Her husband was present there at the lake. I ended up speaking to him, and as we spoke, he asked me if there was any way he could help me. He ended up inviting me to be on the local radio show, which had about two million people listening to it every morning. Can you imagine? Who would have thought I would find such a fantastic opportunity at a funeral?

Anyway, he introduced me as the finance expert of Atlanta in that show, and I had only been out of corporate America for barely two months. Obviously, that opportunity produced massive momentum in my career, and I will always be grateful to him for providing me that chance. I could have been nervous or simply denied his offer, but I chose to take it. So, learn to take advantage of opportunities while you can. Opportunities don't knock at your door often, so open the 'freaking' door before they slip away.

Now, you know why I emphasize to look at those most abandoned or unlikely places. They often hide the best diamonds in the town. There were multiple situations where I was not expecting, or not even looking for, opportunities that came out of those situations. Those are the diamonds that I found in the most abandoned places. Therefore, we must often ensure that we are looking in every nook and cranny to find those diamonds.

We must take every operation seriously, even the ones that do not look appetizing or appealing to most people because I always feel like that's where your most exceptional opportunities are going to be. This will be where you can find that diamond because it is also the place where no one else is looking. This is the point where you are breaking the rules, and that is what makes a difference. You will not return empty-handed.

SET GOALS

The most important question at this point is, do you even want those diamonds? We often do things because we want to be a part of the race. But trust me, if you are only doing it because everyone else is doing it, chances are that you are lost. Therefore, it is essential to have a firm goal because it serves as a map for you to follow.

Setting goals helps trigger new behaviors, guides your focus, and sustains that momentum in life. Goals also promote a sense of self-mastery and help you align your focus. In other words, it enables you to focus on the right things. It serves as strong motivation that you must achieve whatever you want in life, even if it is as rare as diamonds.

The point I am trying to make is that it is imperative to set goals that define your priorities. When you have a strong goal, it gives birth to an even stronger burning desire, which is quite healthy for your end goal. This desire, in turn, helps you find your acres of diamonds without giving up. You know you have set the right goal when you wake up every day excited to work toward it. Hence, you must know where your heart is before setting a goal.

Begin with the end in mind.
~ Stephen Covey

SHIFT YOUR FOCUS

From the moment you decided that this is my goal, every action that you take must reflect that objective. It should bring you closer to your goal. So, stop and ask yourself, is your daily routine bringing you any closer to your target? Nothing in your life will change if you do not change yourself.

It is comforting and quite easy to hear those motivational speeches or read motivational books. But what are you actually doing to overcome your lethargy and start working toward your goal's success? You have set your goal, you have the starting point and a destination to reach. Now, it's time to set your priorities and shift your focus.

It is easy to get distracted on the way if you do not have a strong goal and a burning desire. So, to stay focused, write down your goals. Create a mission statement. Read it to yourself as a reminder every day if you find it hard to stay focused. It will also help you decide where you need to invest your time and energy. Remember, working smart is better than working hard. It's better to invest in the right place rather than in a dead end. What do you value? What do you believe in? What do you want to achieve or accomplish? How are you doing things differently than others? Answer these questions, and you will have your mission statement.

Always remember, your focus determines your reality.
~ George Lucas

DO NOT GIVE UP!

What an overly-used, underrated statement! When used at the right time and spoken in the right tone, these four words can motivate anyone to get up, wipe the dust off, and continue to fight. Your goal must be exciting enough to keep you motivated and not give in to a minor inconvenience.

Remember, you are seeking diamonds; they are rare. The ones that hold value are even rarer, so keep digging. Maybe the moment you decide to stop digging is the moment where you were only an inch away from finding your acres of diamonds! Now, at this point, you must know you are not greedy. You are just a passionate, hard worker who works day and night to achieve his goals.

Nobody said it was going to be easy. There will be moments where you want to cry, moments where you want to scream your lungs out, and moments where your entire body will hurt because you have been too hard on yourself. But believe me, in the end, it's all worth it!

Just do not lose faith in your goal and stay true to yourself. Do the right thing, and do not let the 'fire of desire' fade. Remember, you wrote a mission statement! Fuel that fire by repeating that in your head. Write it on a piece of paper and stick it at a spot you happen to see every day. It will help you stay motivated and focused on achieving your goal and not give in.

Your progress may be slow, but that does not mean you are not progressing. Just never lose faith. Believe that you have already achieved your goal, and soon, you will! The things I just talked about are the traits of the most successful people in this world. How else do you think they achieved their goals?

Even Thomas Edison made 1,000 unsuccessful attempts before he finally invented the bulb. So, who do you think you are? I know this is quite an outdated example, but it never fails to motivate the person reading or hearing it. Always remember your self-worth, and never say that you cannot do something. There is nothing in this world that you cannot do if you have a desire strong enough.

Thomas Edison's teachers said, *"He was too stupid to learn anything."* He was even fired from his first two jobs for being non-productive. Maybe he knew he didn't belong there. He always knew he was made to do something bigger than himself. No, I am not asking you to do something as extravagant as inventing the bulb. I am only asking you not to give up on the goals you have set for yourself, no matter how big they are!

At the end of this chapter, I leave you with a reminder:

TAKE NO OPPORTUNITY FOR GRANTED.

Set a goal and invest yourself completely in that goal. You will never fail until you believe that you have! Do not listen to what other people have to say and keep moving in the direction of your dreams. It may seem impossible at the moment, but soon, you will find your acres of diamonds. All you need to do is stay focused, and work on it every single day of life, one step at a time.

> *I didn't fail 1000 times. The light bulb was an invention*
> *with 1000 steps.*
> ~ Thomas A. Edison

About Felipe

Born in Atlanta, Georgia, Felipe Barganier is a self-made entrepreneur who boasts of nearly 20 years of experience in the corporate insurance and financial services industries. Starting his career in 1999, he took a position in the back office of a broker-dealer firm and excelled. During his time there, he took and passed the General Securities Representative Exam (Series 7), enabling him to obtain his broker's license. After gaining that credential, he went on to work for two larger firms, focused on asset management and insurance benefits. The skills and expertise gained from those firms allowed him to climb the corporate ladder, earning a promotion as the Public Sector Manager for the State of Georgia and various sales and production awards.

Inspired by Richard Branson's billion-dollar entrepreneurial portfolio, in 2003, Felipe stepped out on his own and opened the doors of GAB International, LLC—an insurance, employee benefits, retirement benefits, and payroll provider. In the competitive employer benefits industry, Barganier is one of the only African-American founders of a successful benefits brokerage firm. In addition to providing a superior product, the company's mission focuses highly on the business consumer experience.

Since becoming an entrepreneur, he has been recognized by multiple organizations and has received public honors, including the 2016 Georgia Minority Business Insurance Industry Of The Year Award and the 2017 BenefitsPRO Broker of the Year finalist (top 5). Since its inception, GAB International, LLC, has held a prominent presence in its home state, nationally, and as of 2018, globally. In 2017, he was featured on the cover of BenefitsPRO Magazine and was deemed part of the industry's "winners circle." Also, in 2017, he co-authored the bestselling book, *Breaking Through The Status Quo*—a compilation of industry best practices and influential advice to guide business owners toward saving revenue and paying less for quality benefits. The book was well-received, and impressive sales led to further credibility of the GAB International brand.

Those successes sparked global business travel for the serial entrepreneur as he mapped out the blueprint for the international expansion of the firm, its product offerings, and client base. Additionally, he joined the ranks of elite thought leaders and employee benefits advisors in the country, through the NextGen Benefits Mastermind Partnership group. With the surge in personal brand momentum growing, the demand for Felipe to serve on panels and join motivational speaking stages increased. Because of his dedication to educating others, Felipe keeps his community footing secure with memberships at 100 Black Men of America, The Commerce Club, Atlanta Business League Economic Committee, and various volunteer organizations.

A family man at heart, the father of three enjoys fatherhood more than any other position in his life. His two sons and daughter are the nucleus of his motivation and the root of his desire to form a strong legacy. Seeing his children as future leaders, he leads by positive example and spends quality time pouring into their interests with them.

When he is not spending time with family or focused on business matters, you can find him volunteering, cooking, in the front row at a boxing match, or working on his next book. He is also a certified NLP Coach.

CHAPTER 16

PASSION FOR SUCCESS

BY DR. RAVEE PACKIRISAMY

If I have another chance to do it all over once again, I will not fret. Instead, I will be more excited than ever to replicate the journey. The excitement is knowing that I will have lesser crossroads and fewer bumps to encounter with more wisdom and a higher probability of achieving the same feat in half the time. This reality of life confrontation is happening in everyone's life every time, whether one likes it or not. The natural choice to avoid supersedes the passion to face it all over again.

INNER CHANGE, OUTER RESULTS

On my journey mentoring thousands of individuals from various backgrounds, I always get faced with a question – is it a fallacy or a fact that *I can change my surroundings by changing myself?* The very fact that this question shows up so often simply shows that many people have the misconception that things around them must change before they can change.

How many times have you heard someone saying, I would be the happiest person if only I had a higher paying job, an understanding spouse, a bigger house for my family, a more comfortable car to drive, and an endless list of other external reasons? I bet I am not wrong if you had said these things yourself in the past. That is ok, I have said these things too.

However, when I came to the realization from my inner journey that I need to reverse the flow of that sentence, and then the result will change. It's that simple! I started to put it into practice. I reprogrammed my thoughts, I said that I have a great business that I am happy about, I have an understanding spouse that I am so happy with, I have a very comfortable car that gives me the pleasure of driving with joy. Guess what – everything I was happy for started to manifest and multiply to abundance.

TO RESPOND OR TO REACT

A fundamental reality of life I learnt was that each of my reactions has a counteraction, which is multiple times my reaction. There were many business challenges and business partners' behavioral changes I started to see and experience as I began in my business endeavor. The primary root causes were related to tough business decisions and sensitive financial management for business continuity. Having gone through such challenges before, I had a better understanding and what I thought would be a higher probability of successful resolutions.

On the contrary, I was faced with invalid objections. In the beginning, I started to react to these objections and push my ideas through, but situations became worse. When I started to sit back quietly to reflect within myself, an amazing solution emerged. Having learnt this new technique, I instead chose to respond to conflicting situations, including those self-inflicted, and I found amazing results in my favor.

Having experienced this I became more aware that when I have the full acceptance of a situation or conflict, a positive manifestation was even speedier. When acceptance is weak, I fight within myself, and that causes massive mindset damage within me, further aggravating the situation.

CAN I DEVELOP A PASSION FOR SOMETHING I HAVE NOT EXPERIENCED?

An experience we go through is very personal, it is sometimes very private. Nevertheless, life experiences are the fundamentals in the formation of a wholesome persona. The journey of life experiences begins with the first breath in and ends with the final breath out. In between this reality, it's how I choose to make the best of my journey of experiences. Every experience in life, as far as I am concerned, is new. Therefore, I will see it as new, I will adopt it as new, I will treasure it as new, and I will build my passion on it with an unwavering belief that I can make this new experience an opportunity to build my destiny.

When I accept an experience of failure with a positive mindset, I am then able to see, adapt, treasure, manifest and transform that experience as a fitting tool for my massive success. The experience of a failure is new, but my belief system was bigger than the failure. Hence, using that experience as a steppingstone on my success journey has always been my passionate choice.

GIVERS GAIN

Like most of natures' creation, there is a never ending supply of air for all of us to breath for millions of years. Similarly, water, trees, plants, vegetables, fruits, birds, insects, creatures and the entire natural ecosystem never cease to exist. Does it ever stop its creation because there is overpopulation in this world? Does it ever say I will stop giving because people abuse and do not appreciate it? Nature is ever-giving, ever-forgiving, ever-ready to be sacrificed without resistance.

How did I get connected?

As I was facing great challenges in my journey through my encounters with unappreciative people or abusive characters, I started to seclude myself in the surroundings of nature to calm my thoughts and feelings. That's where I began to observe the freshness or the nature and the calmness of the deep blue sea, the freedom of the animals and the beautiful sounds of birds and insects. I started to ask myself what do they have in common with human beings? They are not disturbed by the destruction caused by humans; they are able to adapt to any situation and yet still continue to contribute to the ecosystem – made up of predators and prey. My realization of becoming a giver to humanity started to become clearer and more meaningful. The significance of my existence became more apparent. I started to experience that the more I give, the more I get back in many unimaginable ways blessed by the universe. Nature taught me yet another valuable lesson.

THE BEST IS ALREADY WITHIN ME, TAP IT

Contented is a word that's literally not in my vocabulary. To me, being contented would stop my creative thinking process, stunt my inspirational growth and make me a sedentary person, which would lead to a premature end to my life's journey.

When I say "The best is yet to come" in any of my speeches, or to anyone interviewing me for media or talk shows, I mean what I say. Do you know what the definition is of the best? If there is something that we can do better than what we did today, then how can we say we have done the best? Best is beyond excellence and beyond outstanding. Therefore, I always believe I can do better. This is my consistent message to anyone within my business or social circle. I express this message in many ways, through words and actions, theory and practical, coaching, and also showing it myself.

If I can believe that I possess abundance of energy within me that I can tap whenever I want, then this philosophy of "the best is yet to come" will readily manifest into a 'gigantic genie' to fulfill all my expectations.

DUALITY

The connotation of duality can sometimes be seen in a negative perspective. While duality is a reality of life, the wisdom to use this **Law of Duality** in a positive manner lies in an individual with proper guidance.

I realize that as a human, we experience many mixed emotive moments like happiness and sadness, anxiety and confidence, acceptance and rejection, triumph and disappointment. These are great feelings and I am thankful to God that I am blessed with the aptitude to accept them as my part of life.

A master once told this beautiful story to a boy who asked, "Why sometimes people are good, but the same people who are good are sometimes bad. How can this be?"

To this the master said, "Inside each one of us, there are two wolves, one is a good wolf and one is a bad wolf. Both these wolves fight." So, the boy thought for a moment and then asked the master, "Master, which wolf wins?" And the master replied, "The one you feed. The one you feed gets stronger and will win."

This story had a deep influence on me. It became crystal clear that if I give attention to negative things, the negativity will manifest in my life. Likewise, if I feed myself with positive and progressive thoughts, then success will become more apparent in me too.

THE UNIVERSAL LAW

We are all aware of the **Law of Cause and Effect**. This has been a fundamental guiding principle in my formative years of doing business, especially when managing very large numbers of people globally. It is far easier to speak the truth because you don't have to create a lie. The truth remains the truth no matter when and where it is repeated. This is unlike creating a lie. A lie is more difficult to withhold or hide as one has to memorize when and to whom it was said. It can take just one slip-up to cause a disaster. This I consider as integrity of the highest order in the business world. The understanding and application of this Universal Law will prevent moral, ethical and business fatalities.

GRATITUDE

In my world of social and business integration, blessed by divine order, I have given very high importance to the attitude of gratitude, which I preach and practice. This habit can change the destiny of any individual. It is a habit that can connect with people at any level of society. The magic I experience within myself is unsurmountable in many ways.

Just be thankful for everything and sometimes even for the most important but the least appreciated thing – like the air we breathe every second of our life. Have we ever been thankful for the highly sophisticated mechanism within our body that works so effortlessly to allow the air to enter our lungs, to provide the gift of life without any conscious effort from birth, without taking a break to rest? When this process stops, it is 'rest in peace' for the body. The least that I can do is to be thankful for the abundance that nature is offering, which protects us and provides for us without any expectation.

I also learnt that being thankful for something that I have set as my goal and yet to achieve is a definite way of allowing it to manifest and becoming a reality. My consistent business progression and expansion has been a gratitude-based visualization and the manifestation of my goals.

EVERYONE CAN BE A STAR

I am simply a conduit to make changes in peoples' lives. It is now my passion to be able to stimulate the awareness within every person I interact with. *My objective is to make each one realize that whatever you want to achieve in life is a matter of aligning the goals with the purpose and passion.* The unwavering alignment and steadfast belief, along with a clear intention of achieving your ambition, will begin to synchronize and you will be surprised to see new paths opening for you, the right tools that you will need appear, and most of all, the Godsent people who will support your mission. One has to stay focused and maintain the trust.

Providing guidance for socially-displaced members of the society, as my corporate social responsibility among many others, has been the conviction of my belief that everyone is a winner by birth. The imprints gathered, be it willingly or unintentionally along life's journey, eventually determine the destiny of the person.

Therefore, ensuring the accumulation of positive imprints like believing in myself, trusting my knowledge and skills and having a clear blueprint of my life, is more likely to give the desired result of a balanced and successful individual.

Everyone is God's child, and everyone has the fullest blessings with divine consecration protecting us at every moment. If one can see and feel the Divine's work in our lives daily, especially at moments of joy or desperation, you will realize that God will not let his perfect creation become a dysfunctional state. Instead, he provides various ways and means to bring his creation to connect to their **Way2Success** with humanity, integrity and love.

About Dr. Ravee Packirisamy

Dr. Ravee Packirisamy, is an entrepreneur, author, trainer and motivational speaker known for his theories on transformation, and an International Training Consultant for Tasly International Co., Ltd. of Tasly Group. He has been the monumental force behind the business expansion of Tasly pharmaceutical healthcare product range, contributing over USD150 million sales turnover in the past 15 years using a network marketing platform. Following his outstanding performance, dedication and tenacity, Tasly Group awarded the exclusive distributorship status for their core products to Jasacare Sdn. Bhd, a company founded by Dr. Ravee. Jasacare today supplies its healthcare product range to various pharmacy chain outlets and wellness outlets throughout the country. His international business expansion over the last decade has created many new business opportunities and affiliations globally.

Dr. Ravee is a renowned speaker for his transformative talks to the direct selling industry around the globe, and a maestro with a passion to transform people by tapping the inner energy within every individual. He is the founder of Way2Sucess Resources, providing trainings and seminars for entrepreneurs and public enrichment programs for the middle and higher education students as well as his corporate social responsibility initiatives for the socially-displaced members of society.

His success journey was no coincidence, nor did it come on a silver platter. As any ordinary working person who comes from a village background, Dr. Ravee had quite the opposite engineering happening within himself. He pursued his goals to **break barriers** and achieve extraordinary success, which he successfully did within 1.5 decades.

Awards and accolades received include: Most Prestigious Outstanding Entrepreneur Award by Asia Pacific Entrepreneurship Award (APEA) in 2007, Corporate Leader(s) of the Year Award in 2009, first Malaysian to have his Footprint embedded in gold at the Star Avenue in Tianjin China in 2006. Honorary Doctorate of Philosophy, Achiever of "The Malaysian Independent Award 1957", the Global Entrepreneur Award from Malaysian Indian Business Association (MIBA) in 2008. He was featured in The Malaysian Indian Journey Book 2010 & Who's Who Constitution, Government and Politics – 2013/14 edition, and Commissioned as Senior Assistant Commissioner of RELA Malaysia (People's Voluntary Corp) by the Malaysian Ministry of Home Affairs.

His high-geared success journey was the prelude to local and international media attention, to which he was invited as a guest speaker on various media channels.

He has captured his vast experiences in many books and audio recordings since 2008. In 2018, Dr. Ravee also co-authored *The Abundance Factor* with world-renowned author, Dr. Joe Vitale, which became an Amazon #1 Best Seller. Dr. Ravee's magical story of using the Law of Attraction in his own life is an inspiration to thousands.

Dr. Ravee is a committee member of Club RELA Kehormat/Bersekutu W.P. and a member of Malaysia Crime Prevention Foundation. Today, Dr. Ravee devotes his initiatives reaching out to people seeking social enhancement, financial transformation, business knowledge and skills development as well as inner growth. The uniqueness of Dr. Ravee's approach in transformative coaching makes him *a star above the rest.*

You can connect with Dr. Ravee at:
- www.facebook.com/raveetaslyglobal.taslyglobal
- Instagram: raveetasly
- YouTube Channel: Way2Success - Dr Ravee
- www.way2success.my
- www.jasacare.com
- www.facebook.com/waytosuccessresources

CHAPTER 17

CONVERSATIONS AND LETTERS AT THE KITCHEN TABLE

BY JULIE MEATES

If you have one gift in your marriage, the father said, 'It is the kitchen table.' It is where problems are shared, and successes celebrated. At that table, there is love, generosity, sharing of food. It is a space where kindness can grow. Around it sits the family. It can be a seedbed of loving family dialogue, and harmony or disharmony.

From the table, one can see the garden with all its metaphors of success. Life is like a garden, within which a wise person is like a flourishing fruit tree. For fruit to grow, the tree needs light, to be nurtured, fed, and pruned back occasionally. All this emerges as symbolism for the bigger picture and jigsaw of life.

Inner talents wait to be woken again, like a beautiful sunrise. Deep down, your intuitive devotion and love for God lives inside, guiding and unconditionally loving you and your potential talent; you are loved by your family and friends. When all the pieces come together – sometimes with frustration – they form a bigger picture. When pieces are missing, we can sometimes search around us though the answer is right under our nose. So too, with our talents: sometimes they are sitting inside us, concealed because of some false belief or vow we have formed, hidden inside us.

Our time on this earth is limited. Every day, on average, we take twenty thousand breaths and originate sixty thousand thoughts; make them good and positive ones. However, the true essence of life is measured not by the number of breaths that we take, but by the moments that take our breath away. As Pope Paul VI said, 'Somebody should tell us, right at the start of our lives, that we are dying. Then we might live life to the limit, every minute of every day. Do it, I say! Whatever you want to do, do it now. Take action. There are only so many tomorrows'.

Etched into the table are phrases, names unknown; seeds sowed. Some of them are like weeds that need pulling as they pop up, so only the desired and beautiful grows. It is up to us to weed the garden of our mind, to replace the weeds with blooms. Some thoughts need erasing and cleaning, but others are like pearls—treasure that feeds the heart and soul.

VOICES AROUND THE TABLE

The kitchen table always has room for hospitality, for another person. Sometimes people are squeezed tightly together to hear and receive gifts and treasure, and all ages are welcome. The table does not discriminate. It goes beyond appearances, although some have more beauty. Martin Luther King's 'I have a Dream' speech lay on it as did unity and diversity. Silent prayers at the table heard; indeed, a candle often lit. Conversation emanates like the sweet smell of blossoms as people listen and genuinely care, or comes like a sharp prickle from a thorny rose.

The kitchen table always has room for a stranger, a friend, a family member. Sometimes, it is hard and woody, and sometimes covered in beauty. It is always there at birthdays, definitely at

Christmas. The table does not argue and is more loyal than the family pet. The table has seen both uncontrollable laughter and a deluge of tears; it is the best keeper of secrets. It never divulges. It speaks not but listens and remembers. It holds pain and heartache, but with a quick clean, the mess is cleared. The kitchen table is easy to protect; it hears the secrets of success.

Sometimes the kitchen table needs sandpaper to smooth the edges. Successful relationships matter. Sometimes those who sit at the kitchen table may rub others like sandpaper, but always allow yourself to be crafted for your life's purpose, to become a work of art, to alchemize lead into gold. There are times when the kitchen table resembles a boxing ring. Remember the rules: Play fair. Play clean. Act with integrity. If you want to be successful, think positive thoughts, as you are much more likely to manifest positive outcomes. Negative thoughts can manifest negative results. Be careful what you focus on, be clear. Negativity can stick. Positive thoughts are crucial.

The kitchen table often has books piled high – *The Secrets of Success; Success Principles* – with messages like: 'take 100% responsibility for your life'. It has listened to the secrets of a good life and heard the trials and tales of the opposite. It has seen the glass shattered and watched the candle burn. Let it burn out any pain to manifest love and joy. It has watched people turn negatives into positives.

The world needs people who are awake, fully conscious, and responsible for their actions. Though it is not always easy to take personal responsibility for our actions, this is an empowering pathway with hope for the future. Be kind with your words wherever possible. Use your words in truth and love. Leave a spark of goodness in the world we go. As Marianne Williamson said in her book, *A Return to Love*, "It is our Light, not our darkness, that most frightens us".

Motivate yourself to find yourself – the core of your being that only you and God know.

Pray, protect, and clear. In the depths of winter, those months of inward reflection—look inside and let go. Sometimes this reflects on the outside. Use good habits, because habits make us, and in the world, we need people with good habits. Cleanliness is next to Godliness. Clean up after yourself, for if the world did this, we would not be in the mess we are in, physically, intellectually, and emotionally. Be responsible for yourself and do the work to get inner health, happiness, and wellness. The answers lie within you as the sky lies beyond you and the Earth grounds beneath you. You are loved, a child of God, no less, no more, for this in itself is miraculous. God makes nothing without worth. He hears your first words and hears your last.

The table has been there to help those who hurt. It has heard about forgiveness and trust. But the greatest successes of the kitchen table are in family togetherness. Love starts in the home and from there emanates to the world. Be true to yourself and remember the simple code: Do unto others that we would want them to do unto us. It is a place where you learn to help; use good manners: 'please' and 'thank you' are the magic words. Start and end each day with a grateful heart. Have conversations on the dreaded F-word. *Reframe* to family, faith, fun, friends, and fitness. Take challenges like Junk Free June or read the book – *One Month To Live: Thirty Days To A No-Regrets Life* by Kerry & Chris Shook.

It is a place of metamorphosis, changing from the inside out. It has witnessed earthquakes and had to learn skills that build a foundation that lasts. When an earthquake or the tsunami of life hits, we find out what we are made of. True colors show under stress. It brings out the good in kindness towards strangers and our fellow man. None of us would dispute that a solid foundation is the key to structural integrity. An unshakable foundation is also key to building a meaningful existence, a lasting marriage, a strong family, a successful business, and even a nation. How can we earthquake-proof our lives, building on the right foundation?

FOOD AT THE KITCHEN TABLE

Conversations start with food – a blessing, gratitude, a thank you for the food we eat and the hands that made it. An Attitude of Gratitude. Conversations around the table remind us that more than 2,000 years ago, Hippocrates, the father of modern medicine, taught us, "Let thy food be thy medicine." Look after your heart and be kind and caring to yourself and others. Eat well, for the body is the temple for your soul. Take exercise.

Clear your space. Clean up your messes and stresses, so beauty and light reflect inside. Mostly believe that you are very loved by us all and that God loves you too. There is enough stress out there without carrying it in ourselves. Love changes everything. Stay connected to God's love inside you as it paves a way that has beauty in the challenges, miracles in the mayhem, and sometimes the madness of life. When you get a chance, the gift may come from helping others through their trials and tribulations. Sometimes, it is the simple pleasures that matter: a meal together, help, cook, clean together.

The table has listened to and discussed Jack Canfield's *Principles of Success*. It has heard about the purposes of your life. What does your life revolve around right now? Who or what is at the center of your life's wheel? It has looked at the Power and Control Wheel and knows that strength lies not in bullying, but equality and respectful, loving relationships. The lesson of non-violence by Gandhi lay on it. He learned the lesson from his wife when he tried to bend her to his will. "Her determined resistance to my will ultimately made me ashamed of myself, and cured me of my stupidity in thinking I was born to rule over her, and in the end, she became my greatest teacher of non-violence." That is success.

The kitchen table also exists at Lake Titicaca, the highest navigable lake in the world, by a simple stove, and hears the success principle of their land: no lying, no stealing, do not be lazy. It has heard of cultures that have succeeded at the expense of others, and greed, and also taught lessons that ensure you give a tenth of your earnings to others. That is success.

THE TABLE AS SHELTER

The humble kitchen table has withstood hurricanes and the winds of change. It has changed addresses, yet we can shelter under it when the earth shakes. It has heard that 90% of effort is attitude. If you do not like something, change it.

> *If you can't change it, change your attitude. Don't complain.*
> ~ Maya Angelou

Their children have listened to Dale Carnegie's Three Cs of success: do not complain, criticize, or condemn. Avoid two D's – defensiveness and denial, and one B – blame. Remember the A's – appreciate, accountability, acceptance, and ask. If you put down, build up. For every put-down, you need to say three things positive to uplift another. Sometimes it even goes to ten. That is magic. It has learned that complaining is draining, that it is better to bless rather than deride, and that Love and Compassion are essential ingredients; without them, there is no humankind.

It has witnessed endless debates, crucial conversations, and 'what if' scenarios. What if someone gave you drugs? What would you do? How would you know how to handle this situation. How to say no to that, not good? Be careful while drinking – say no, or only to the monkey stage, not the peacock, lion, or pig. In addition, don't forget the table is a cell phone-free zone.

One of the most beautiful is the letters that sometimes lie on it: My dearest unique, blessed and loved child, God gave us a most beautiful, divine gift – yes, you were a gift to us from God. Now many years down the road, you are embarking on another journey and chapter in your book of life, love, career, friendship… physically, intellectually, emotionally, and spiritually.

You are adventurous. You are artistic, capturing and releasing such ideas, and beauty on paper with your brother and friend. They still hang inside as a symbol of the color and beauty that exists inside us. Art gives a message – so often a symbolism of hope. You are ambitious, expressing inner stirrings through singing and playing the guitar and piano, and earlier in life writing those songs. Are they still around? Definitely another few songs exist within the realm of your inner goodness, divinely guided.

You are loved and love, ringing with your beautiful messages of love to me; you have incredible timing and incredible love. It takes courage to love. I have still saved them for a rainy day. You have a big heart – a kind heart; even more to respect – respect yourself and others. That is success. A man with a good heart, kind words is a pleasure to the soul. To love and respect your mother is a measure of success.

Even more to love and be positive in love in a fully self-aware way. Know while the road sometimes is paved with gold, it also is paved with mercurial stones that may cause us to stumble, and lose sight of who we are and what we believe. All the positive and abundant blessings, and beautiful values and virtues that are the well-spring of life, exist inside you. Know how to get back quickly on the positive road when challenges exist, and to thyself be true.

Know how to dust off the outer layer of grime so clarity can be crystal clear. Never lose the essence of your soul, because God designed you for a special purpose with unique gifts. Do not bury your talents. Use them to create happiness in your heart and home, first and foremost. So, they can be sprinkled as goodness on a world that needs help and healing. For God is within everyone one of us. The divine essence with which the earth circles the sun exists in you to let your light shine. Know when to shine the light and observe, for sometimes that is only a message from the divine for us. With that observation, there is no judgment.

HAPPINESS

In the end, what matters? How well did you live, how well did you love? And finally, how well did you let go? And in the present moment, with the will of God, everything will be all right. God is watching from a distance. That is success.

Thank you yet again for the beautiful flowers and the message. I want you to know that I love you very much and wish only the best for you. Hasten slowly.

Remember "Desiderata":
'Many fears are born from fatigue and loneliness.'

'Ensure you fill your cup of happiness with love.'

And let the winds of the heavens dance between you.
~ Kahlil Gibran

I wish merely good life for you, inner peace, abundance, good health, love, and happiness for you. Keep your faith, for that is the rock that keeps you strong. Keep close to God, for through Faith is the gentle hand which guides and surpasses all understanding.

This is what lies inside the kitchen table, whether it is a summer's day or a cold, dreary winter's night, whether an earthquake hits or a virus spreads. The kitchen table stands firm, unmoved by the outside world. It is sometimes slightly scratched but always etched with memories. Like life sometimes, what happens there is not always fair, but the situation can still be turned around by looking for the good, the positive. One strength about the kitchen table is it has the four pillars of strength – its four legs represent the pillars of love, the heart, and kindness. Know the fourth leg exists as a combination, and acknowledging us as physical, intellectual, spiritual, and loving emotional beings. Stabilized by a solid surface that is connected, inside is a drawer either empty (meaningless) or filled with the secrets and treasures of life. Remember that.

Live your life like it is your last year on Earth. Live a life of no regrets and remember that in the many successes of life, the one most treasured is your family.

An Attitude of Gratitude:

> "On the other hand, beautiful thoughts of all kinds crystallize into habits of grace and kindliness, which solidify into genial and sunny circumstances: pure thoughts crystallize into habits of temperance and self-control, which solidify into circumstances of repose and peace: thoughts of courage, self-reliance, and decision crystallize into manly habits, which solidify into circumstances of success, plenty, and freedom: energetic thoughts crystallize into habits of cleanliness and industry, which solidify into circumstances of pleasantness: gentle and forgiving thoughts crystallize into habits of gentleness, which solidify into protective and preservative circumstances: loving and unselfish thoughts crystallize into habits of self-forgetfulness for others, which solidify into circumstances of sure and abiding prosperity and true riches."

> ~ James Allen, *As a Man Thinketh.*

About Julie

Julie Meates is a New Zealand-born humanitarian endeavouring to bring more peace, kindness and love into our world. Her career has been multifaceted and varied. For her, family has been important. She is married with three wonderful children and a wide, diverse, extended family.

Julie has a passion for education and health starting her early career as a teacher. She has also qualified as a social worker, counselor and is now a barrister and solicitor, and is currently involved in post-graduate work in education and health. She is passionate about community well-being and has worked in a volunteer capacity in many roles – with the mantra and hope that kindness will be paid forward.

In 2002, she was the co-founder of the Fulfil A Dream Foundation with a vision of strong and happy families, strong and vibrant communities and wise and visionary leadership – empowering individuals, family and communities. Fulfil A Dream Foundation was fortunate to work with high profile musicians, sportsmen, politicians, community, education and health leaders. Julie was also the chairperson of a Maori learning centre (indigenous Kohanga reo).

Currently, Julie is a volunteer with community law's programme of community justice panels. The Community Panel process aims to repair the harm caused by the offender promptly, using restorative justice processes. She has been a volunteer on United Nations executive in her Canterbury region as Board Secretary, and presently with the inception of Women of Hope Wake up, and Help Ourselves Trust Board.

She has been involved over the years with Women's Refuge and several other NGO/charitable institute non-governmental organisations – COGS (Community Organisation Grants Scheme). She was vice president of International Community Organisation (Wairarapa International Communities Incorporated) Society, and was involved in community radio doing local, national and international broadcasts. She has also worked with the homeless nationally and internationally.

Julie has been part of many community lead initiatives to strengthen communities, in sometimes complex situations, weaving together storytelling and music, and empowering youth and community talent.

She has represented sport and has coached at high school, as well as being a physical education and health teacher and tutor; and she has further qualifications in design. In her high school, she was awarded best all-round person.

Julie Meates is a quiet leader, able to inspire, influence, coordinate and empower people to achieve desired goals. Julie is experienced in working in partnership with organisations, with local communities and individuals to make a difference. She is empathetic, positive, non-judgmental and kind, with an ability to relate to a wide range of people.

CHAPTER 18

WHERE BELIEF BLOOMS

BY RACHEL WITHERS

Wildflowers grow at different rates. The blue lupine shoot straight toward the sky. The daisies burst onto the scene in clusters of white or yellow, shorter than the lupine, but beautiful in their own way. Each flower grows in its own manner, in its own time, and focuses solely on its own progress. The daisy doesn't quit because it will never be as tall as the lupine. Flowers stretch out into the sunshine, thankful for each ray and every raindrop. Wildflowers are especially resilient, as they often grow in unattended plots of soil.

Humans should grow like wildflowers.

As many people do, I learned to grow like a wildflower the hard way. During my early career in dance, I allowed weeds—well-meaning directors and agents—to obscure my sunshine. Today, as a Personal Empowerment and Business Strategist, my mission is to help you become the success you are meant to be. I use what I learned through my own journey to help others blossom personally and professionally.

Dance found me at age five. It came naturally to me, so I danced with passion and for the enjoyment of it. I attended The Royal Ballet School and later danced on stage professionally, during which time self-doubt took center stage, and passion and enjoyment were forced into the stage wings. I was short for a dancer in an era when George Balanchine's New York City Ballet influenced dance everywhere with tall, long-limbed creatures against which every other dancer was measured. I allowed others' opinions to crush my dream bit-by-precious-bit. The dance world, especially, can bruise a person's ego. Well-meaning casting directors comment on dancers' weight, height, and shape. They even suggest plastic surgery to correct imperfections. Can you imagine? It is all too easy to let doubt creep in. The more I allowed those thoughts space in my head, the more I became introverted and lost confidence.

From that experience, I gained insight that became the foundation on which I have built my businesses. If it's in your head, it's a dream; if it's truly in your heart, a passion; and then you can have it in your hand, a reality. Dream. Passion. Reality. Taking a dream and passion and manifesting them into your reality does not happen haphazardly. It requires thought, action, and practice.

Consider your mind as a flower garden. The seeds you sow in the garden—the thought patterns you allow—grow in your subconscious mind. Nurturing thoughts: I am good enough, I am, I will, I trust, I believe, and I will make it, are thoughts of power and conviction. Negative thoughts are the weeds. Negative thoughts such as, I am not good enough, I am not talented enough, I am not clever enough, and I am never going to make it, choke the power of the subconscious mind. Personal and professional growth bloom in a garden that is regularly tended and fed positive, focused thoughts. We have to remove the negative, hurtful, and self-limiting thought patterns.

Long before a seed begins to grow into a flower, the essence of what it will become lives inside it at its core. Outer influences like rain, sun, and nutrients help what is already inside the seed to grow. Humans, too, grow from the inside out. What they will become has everything to do with the spirit that moves within them. This is the spirit of things, the passion for something that resides so deep that it becomes one with every action a person takes.

Always pursue your passion, because when you pursue a passion, you do things for the right reasons. Never chase money. Money can be a happy by-product of pursuing your passion, but it cannot become your passion. If you are working at something about which you are passionate, you become more valuable, you serve better, and you usually become more successful. You're not thinking about bank balances. You're thinking, *"What value as an individual can I contribute?"* Ultimately, your attitude toward life is the attitude that will come back at you. Live out your passion and add value to the world. You will tear yourself apart if you are not doing the things you love and for which you are passionate. People believe more strongly and think more positively about the things for which they are passionate.

Beliefs are self-limiting. What you think becomes the action you take. If you believe you can achieve something, you can! Your beliefs and self-talk shape your ability to realize your goals and create the life you desire. No amount of hard work or determination will lead to success and fulfilment if your beliefs aren't aligned with your dreams and your passions. If you believe you will fail, you will. Consider the placebo effect, for example. A person takes a pill that has no real medicinal benefit; however, they respond to the "treatment." Scientists have offered one possible reason for the placebo effect—expectation. When a person expects the pill to work, the body's own chemistry does the rest. Negativity is all the weeds.

The relationship you have with your mind ultimately is the relationship you have with yourself. Remind yourself that your mind is neither good nor bad; your mind is what you choose to make it. Any time you hesitate to take the next step toward your dream, take a moment to notice why you hesitate to make the phone call, send the email, or decide not to go for a run today.

Were you thinking, "What if they don't reply? What if I fail?" We place the obstacles "yeah but," "but if," and "if only" in our own paths to stop ourselves from moving forward.

Begin with gratitude as the foundation into which you will plant every other thought. Start from a place of gratitude for what you have, and the positive energy associated with gratitude will boost every other action you take toward achieving your goals. Plants are thankful for each drop of water and ray of sunshine; they make the best use of it. Gratitude sets you up for success; then, you act.

The actions you take are what will nurture the garden of your mind. You've certainly heard that talking to plants will make them grow stronger. If plants respond to positive affirmations, imagine how strong you will grow in your goals when showered with positivity.

Why, then, do we listen to other people's voices over our own?

It is curious.

We dream about something our whole life and then squash that dream because someone we might have met five minutes ago said, "Oh, I don't think you should be doing that." They don't know us. They don't know about our grand plan, but sometimes we listen to them. Why do we do that? We often listen to others because we compare our journey with their journey. We assume that if they are successful, they must have the one right way of doing things. Remember, a sunflower doesn't compare itself with the other sunflowers. It doesn't look around and think, "I'm not the tallest sunflower, so I should stop growing." Flowers are not concerned with the other flowers; they simply reach for the sun.

One simple action I encourage clients to take to nurture the garden of their mind is to record themselves speaking as if they have already achieved their goal. If their goal is to become a successful author, then they will record themselves stating, "I am a best-selling author. I am grateful to have sold 100,000 copies of my book." Playing back the recording, hearing about their own success, connects them to the spirit of the thing they are on their way to achieving. Written affirmations are another nurturing strategy. The written word is wonderfully powerful. When you write something down, your brain commits to it because the mind knows only what you tell it. Posting those affirmations in a location that will frequently be seen further solidifies the thought. What you tell yourself most of the time is what your subconscious mind acts upon. Your subconscious mind does not differentiate between reality and imagination. It takes what you tell yourself and works to create that reality.

Once you have committed your brain to the journey, you practice.

Practice mindfulness to become a master gardener of your mind. Mindfulness is a type of meditation that involves breathing methods, guided imagery, and other practices to relax the mind and body and reduce stress. To practice mindfulness, you develop a regular meditation practice to strengthen the areas of the brain that control awareness and emotions. Through this, you gain a greater understanding of your thoughts and emotions, allowing you to identify the thoughts that are holding you back. You only move towards outcomes that you believe to be possible. Belief is more important than talent, ability, and skill set. A person with average talent who believes in themselves, will move toward their goals and fight everything for their dream. Usually, they achieve more than a talented person who lacks belief.

Practice persistence and maintain absolute focus. Focus on your growth and your journey. We tend to see other people's successes, not their failures before they succeeded. Overnight sensations usually aren't that at all. They are people who practiced for success every day, year after year until they finally fulfilled their dream. There might be fifty steps on your journey, and you must take all fifty of them to get there. Acknowledge the achievement of each step that you take on your journey, and you will enjoy the process more.

Practice resilience. It is our setbacks and obstacles which teach us resilience. Resilience enables us to rise above daily challenges repeatedly. A critical change occurs when "if" becomes "how." Whatever path you're on, problems are sure to arise. Instead of pondering if you will solve them, instead, change your mindset to ask yourself, "How will I deal with this challenge?" When you hear yourself begin to say, "I can't," stop and reframe your thoughts. Think instead, "I am able. I will fix this. I can achieve this," rather than, "I don't think I can." These exercises alter the neurotransmitters in the brain, changing the connections so that you have a more positive, proactive approach to your life and your goals. Realize that every setback is a lesson. What can you take from it? Learn, then press on. Any successful gardener will tell you that much of what they know, they learned through trial and error.

Practice gratitude. Gratitude is the foundation of success, and it enriches the soil where success is planted. It is easy to be grateful for the good things that happen on our journey, but we must also practice gratitude for the setbacks we encounter, as well. For every challenge or obstacle, be grateful for the lesson it taught.

SUMMARY

Most people quit when life gets challenging. Those who believe and trust in themselves will succeed because they won't stop until they do. That's the power of self-belief. Change your actions to support your belief. Change your belief, and you change your reality. "I am" are two exceedingly powerful words. What you put after them shapes your life. I am good enough. I am equipped to do this.

Now, ask yourself, "Do I really want to attain my dream?"

If the answer is yes, keep these things in mind as you start to blossom into the person you want to become. The things you believe lead to your actions, and your actions create your reality.

Whatever you want in life can be achieved. You can't control what the world is going to do to you, but you can control how you react. You control your attitude. When emotions become overwhelming, threatening your attitude, take a few moments, and breathe. Clear your thoughts. Once you remind yourself that your attitude is entirely up to you, you can quickly return to the growth mindset path to success, and watch your dreams and your life bloom.

About Rachel

Rachel Withers helps people around the world make mindset and lifestyle changes needed to achieve their dreams.

As a business strategist, serial entrepreneur, and public speaker, Rachel applies her experience to coach clients towards personal empowerment and thriving careers. She is the founder of the successful fitness concept, BalletBeFit, owner of a successful property company, and founder and CEO of the Rachel Withers Academy.

After founding the successful fitness concept, BalletBeFit, Rachel has used her experience to encourage others. Through her courses, Rachel teaches personal development, mindset, wealth mastery, and business development to help each client gain control of their health, wellbeing, career, and finances. As a public speaker, she captivates audiences around the world with tried and tested strategies for empowerment and growth. Rachel supports people as they build a sense of confidence and learn to apply it within their private and public lives.

Rachel is an Amazon #1 bestselling author, with books *Become a FITPreneur, Millionaire Mindset, Make Your Dreams A Reality*, and *Ballet Body*, each written to inspire readers to achieve their goals. She combines her expertise in these areas with a mindful approach to pair clients' goal setting with a sense of awareness that helps them fully enjoy each step of the journey.

Rachel is a former ballerina, trained with the Royal Ballet, and holds a Bachelor of Performance Arts from Leeds University. She has studied and worked with numerous notable dancers, teachers, and choreographers, including Dame Alicia Markova, Vassilie Trunoff, Dame Beryl Grey, and Brenda Last.

When Rachel's dance career ended and she became a mum, her self-esteem took a hit. She realised she needed to make a change for both herself and her family. By transforming her mindset, she used her dance background to develop the ballet-based fitness method, BalletBeFit. This mental shift allowed her to surpass career and fitness goals, inspire women to build businesses, and teach her techniques to students worldwide.

On her path to success, Rachel has worked with incredible mentors such as Pat Mesiti and Bob Proctor. She continues harnessing the insights she learned along the way by creating dynamic content for her followers. She hosts the monthly series Mindset Matters on the Success Channel, which has top speakers such as Brian Tracy, Jack Canfield, and Nick Nanton, and uses her experiences and personal development as a way to connect with audiences at her inspirational public speaking engagements.

Rachel believes we all have what it takes to live the life we deserve. She uses the lessons of her journey to deliver quick results, help readers discover their personal power, and surpass their visions of success. Through Rachel's books and resources, people will learn how to accelerate their progress and self-worth through the power of transforming their mindset.

Connect with Rachel at:
- info@rachelwithershq.co.uk
- www.rachelwithershq.co.uk
- www.twitter.com/rachelwitherhq
- www.facebook.com/rachelwithershq
- www.instagram.com/rachelwithershq
- www.youtube.com/c/RachelWithersHQ

CHAPTER 19

THE GLORY OF FAILURE, THE SORROW OF SUCCESS

BY KATIA STERN

It's incredibly easy to get caught up in an activity trap, in the busy-ness of life, to work harder and harder at climbing the ladder of success only to discover it's leaning against the wrong wall.
~ Stephen Covey

Please enter the beautiful world of energetical embodiment that my mind likes to call success:

- Where your perception of divine perfection has always been in front of your loving soul.
- Where your ego is embraced throughout the temptation of being someone else's idea of cultural triumph, that we like to call success in our society.

For some pleasant and odd reason, I recall a visual portrayal on TV, where I was amazed by this young prodigy, who was participating in a spelling contest. His persona got framed into my mind as a synonym for hyperintelligence and the cultural status-quo for success. I'd just arrived in Canada from Moscow, Russia – where nobody believes in tears, and I was a loved girl to a wealthy father who was a part of the ''successful'' 1% of the system where everything is ruled by the hierarchy.

Success with two C's and a double S.

It seemed like this young man was a genius and could spell long and, back then, such exotically-sounding English words, and paint rainbow-like verbal images that still haven't left my memory lane. Be the way, half of the lingo he used is still mysterious to me. But now, I don't try to make sense of everything. I became very selective about the nature of information, thoughts, emotions, and possibly even frequencies, so that I let my consciousness upload into my operating system…my B.S.,—my belief system. This different type of B.S. dictates almost everything that we think, feel, and do daily in a continuous pattern and unlimited amount.

Little did I know back then, of how much use – practical, emotional, and financial, I would get out of knowing how to spell S-U-C-C-E-S-S.

1. Spell and live by it.
2. Spell and create it.
3. Spell and teach it to others.

Spelling is one thing. But what is the real definition and meaning of success? What is it that we all strive for? What is it that we want? And what is it that we truly need? Unfortunately, when most people claim they want success, they have no clue what it means to them.

We talk about it, we work for it, we fight for it and sometimes even kill ourselves for it, like the promised paradise that some have created in their mind as the radical result of a different kind of success.

We pretend to know what we're doing, trying to live up to the knowledge, expectations, and experiences of our role models: parents, teachers, friends, TV, and most of all our EGO, of course. (Yeah, I used all CAPS for your EGO just so it doesn't feel left out.) "You must get a University degree and you'd better move and groove to the dull sounds of traditional education, otherwise you have a good chance of becoming that University's janitor..."

As a young and rebellious teenager, one that Mr. Marx would put in his communism blueprint as the archetype for a sense of national pride in children, I proudly replied that, in the Soviet Union, all professions are valued, and all people are appreciated and treated equally. My parents rolled their eyes.

Funnily enough, mindset programming works perfectly well for us as well as against us. We grow and think in the same genetically-inherited mindset. And since life is so ironic and simple, we all become diverted, and possibly, better versions of our parents, as I still catch myself saying the same things to my daughter. She is different from me; she is a Canadian teenager. But guess what? She responds with the same attitude... the same energy and the same rebellion. Don't tell her, but I will not lose sleep over this if she chooses her own standard of real success as I did much later in life.

Nowadays, my only measure of being successful is being happy. That's it. I'm happy that I've overcome the embodied paradigm that success should involve struggle – suffering in a constant battle that never ends. I can finally enjoy the fulfillment of living passionately, without having to feel guilty and apologetic about my own deepest desires and impulses that have always been there, no matter how 'badass' or bold they can be.

In my movie, called life, the credits roll and I'm coming out on a scene as a Russian immigrant, having come to Canada by myself, at 17, wearing the highest black lacquer stilettos that were available in the shadowy and corrupt scene of soviet consumerism.

Coming from a wealthy, and by communist standards, successful family, the immigration made me stronger by giving me a role-play of the waitress who had to smile and be grateful for every 25 cent tip the precious men would leave me from a $2.75 beer.

Inside, I was ready to explode, there was so much pain, so much feeling of humiliation. I was holding myself back from becoming part of Charlie Manson's family agenda and completely losing it, because of the lack of respect and empathy I experienced from the drunk, lost souls who approached me on a daily basis. Thank God, I figured out how to use that energy wisely and turned this pain into a self-paced course on anger management that prepared me for all the trials and tribulations of my future life.

I like to think that for all that suffering, life decided to reward me with the role of a 1990's wealthy Monaco resident with a nice "I've made it!" attribute – a young and handsome man who came with a Ferrari and a Yacht as a nice bonus. As if that was not enough (and is it ever enough?) I was offered the role of an American lawyer and got my Master of Laws degree from Miami University.

But as I was getting more experienced (some may call it older, but we know that we are forever young) success started having a different meaning. It had shifted somewhat from the outside world into the inner. It has become a feeling of contentment, an emotion of satisfaction and excitement, a regular experience of ecstatic self-worth.

Like an energizer bunny, but a little sexier, I kept going and going, achieving and overachieving, getting my dopamine and longing for more and more. No time to breathe, stop and think. No time to save for self-talk. No time to hear an honest answer.

— When are you going to be enough?
— When are you going to acknowledge your value and celebrate success?
— Will this be in numbers? ...amount of money? ...degrees? ...skills? ...clients? ...men? ...women who so sweetly envy you?
— What is the true measure of my success?

I got stuck in my own life. I had to stop jolting awake in the middle of the night thinking "OMG! I'm 40, and my life is wasted on a different kind of B.S."

So, I had all the attributes of success and a long list of accolades. Let's check to ensure I am not deceitful to you and it's not my ego speaking:

- Four university degrees
- International best-selling author
- CEO of a personal development business
- A real estate investor
- National-level fitness bikini competitor
- Health coach
- Success coach
- Mother of a talented teenager
- Mrs. Globe beauty pageant participant, and, worth mentioning, very attractive woman

. . . And modest, as you can tell.

I am 47 now. Feeling open and happy about it is another success of mine. Having overcome immense fear of aging, I escaped becoming "formerly hot" and allowed to live my 20s in the 40s.

After all that short story made long, *how would I define success?*

— Was it when I was standing on that yacht, overlooking the curious bystanders, jealously gazing at me? Almost every little girl would want to live that princess-of-the-world dream in the creme de la creme of society with haute couture outfit and jewels, lots of those.
— Then, how about those tears under my fancy sunglasses, when I felt so disastrously lonely?
— Was it that law degree, when at the graduation they said that we were only 2% of the population who "made it"? Being a lawyer is one of the most desired, but hard-to-achieve professions. But how good is that degree if I dreaded the thought of having to go to the

law office every day and spend days doing research, billing, like a woman with low social responsibility, for my hours?
— Or was it the bodybuilding medal?
— Multiple income streams?
— Succeeding as a good mother, perhaps?

Having made a decision to find that true meaning, all of a sudden I started to receive opportunities. Real and unbelievable coincidences that made me question reality.

But I don't believe in coincidences, so meeting one of the great hyper intellectuals of our times, Mr. Bob Proctor himself, was not random.

I mean, how often do you have dinner with somebody from the movie "Secret" that changed your life? Well, I did it twice. Bob Proctor and Jack Canfield. I take those two meetings as a calling to get on a mission. I asked Bob Proctor – Bob, what do I do to become like you, when I grow up? He said: "Write a book, Katia, write a book!" Of course, it was like a splinter in my mind, so I listened to the man who emanates knowledge and trust in such a high frequency. So, two years later, "You were born Wow" got published, and voila, it's a bestseller!

I was not supposed to be in Santa Barbara on the day I met Jack Canfield, but I was. I was not supposed to be invited to that event, but I was. I was not supposed to be one hour early at Jack's event, mess up time and meet him outside the venue, but I did. My inner voice commanded: "Katia, go up to him and ask the same question as you asked Bob!" Again, he said to write a book.

Since my first book was almost done, like a femininely obedient and loyal student, I listened to him and decided to "kill two birds with one stone." Actually, I didn't want to kill anybody, but wanted to write a second book, and get closer to someone who I genuinely believe is a related spirit, someone that has experienced the universal message and understanding on a brighter level.

It felt so related to Jack's experience and expertise in my own selfish good way; so I can spread the love back to you and feel like I am supposed to feel – successful!

So, a year later, I am a Certified Jack Canfield Success Principle Trainer, and the co-author of our beloved and sanctified book – *Success.*

Don't get me wrong, joyfully sharing this about my personal achievements is not something I view as a necessity to influence someone. The message is not to show off what I have, but to share with you how to have it. How to free yourself from yourself, so that you could have an unbelievably amazing journey to becoming truly successful.

However, until you get clear on what success is to you, you will be sitting in that car with no one behind the wheel, even though that little V8, like the astrological infinity, is running so sexily and smoothly. Even if you have a self-driving Tesla, she still needs that final destination entered before the ride – to serve her mastermind to a purposeful satisfaction.

Take a break in your so busy schedule and define your success. What is really for you?

What has to happen so that you can honesty declare to the Universe: "And the Oscar goes to me! I am successful! Hi Mama, I am the happiest university custodian of my mind!" Live your life like you're the hero in your movie.

Until you realize what you fear, and what you desire, you may never get the joy and satisfaction that you are longing for. Until you get rid of inner conflicts, anxiety and overwhelm, there is a chance that you may never get from your "now" to "wow".

Start talking to yourself. Get aware of your reality, are you successful, happy, satisfied?

Self-talk and being true to ourselves is so powerful, yet extremely challenging. You may realize you are living in a box, even if it looks like a golden cage. Being in this golden enclosure does not make you feel successful if deep inside you prefer silver. Or if you want to fly away not to make your mama bird happy, but because you really want it.

You may realize the harsh but awakening truth – Success is a feeling. It's an emotion. It's a state, a state of satisfaction and joy. *The ecstasy of living is real success.* Everyone has equal rights and privileges to sense it. Go ahead, allow yourself!

- ♦ And, just a friendly reminder: You were born Wow!
- ♦ Claim it. Own it. Be Wow.

With lots of love and gratitude,
Katia Stern

P.S. Let me know about your success journey. (See email address in my Bio.) What if we can ride it together? What if? What if? One thing I can promise – it will be fun! Because life is a party. A success party it is!

About Katia

Katia Stern was born and raised in Moscow, Russia and moved to Canada when she was 17. She has since lived in Toronto, Miami, Monaco, Moscow and other countries due to her hunger for new experiences and interests in diverse lifestyles and cultures. She is a single mother of a gifted teenage daughter.

She calls herself a personal development junkie who has always been interested in figuring out how to live the best life possible. She went from a Psychology major to getting a master's in International Law, but found her true purpose to be mentoring ambitious, already successful, accomplished women to get them to the next level of success through inner joy and fulfilment. She has become a health coach, fitness nutrition and hormone specialist, fitness trainer and national level fitness bikini competitor, so that she could help women transform both their bodies and minds.

Later, she became a Certified Jack Canfield trainer in Success Principles, and is now mentoring women all over the world. She is using her extensive list of accolades to help women over forty who have been too busy achieving and overachieving and are now ready to finally start living for themselves. She is empowering them to release all limitations, change their mindsets and old programming, so that they can unleash their true self, get out of overwhelm, feelings of guilt and resentment, and fall in love with themselves, fulfilling their own bold desires and living in peace.

She is an international best-selling author of a book, *You Were Born WOW*. As a firm believer that all of us were born 'WOW' – free, adequate and enough, she is examining how we've been convinced by society, teachers, and parents to think otherwise, and gives simple steps on how to get away from the imprisonment of those old thoughts and beliefs, without having to waste another day on BS.

Her mission, using her energy and passion, is to inspire and motivate women to experience love and joy every day of their lives so that they can have a totally 'Wow life' – vibrant and fulfilling! She is leading by example, and is now participating in the Mrs. Globe Beauty Pageant for women over 45. She is Mrs. Ontario Classique, and is going for the Mrs. Canada Classique title.

Katia calls all her clients 'Stars.' She thinks we are all starring in our movie called life, where we should play the main role and get to choose where to shoot the next scene and who to choose as supporting actors. Also, we are all deserving of our own Oscar! Her Stars call her the "Wow Woman Creator" because she is helping women create a new life – the life of real 'Wow woman!'

Contact information:
- www.Katiastern.com

CHAPTER 20

THE 5-STEP STRATEGY HIGH-ACHIEVING WOMEN LEADERS USE
TO NEGOTIATE LIFE SUCCESS ON THEIR OWN TERMS

BY DR. MONIQUE Y. WELLS

—Are you a spirited, generous, and compassionate high-achieving woman leader?

—Are you the only woman in your professional environment or personal network who has achieved your level of success?

—Do you feel isolated, lonely, and perhaps even guilty, about your success?

I'm Monique Y. Wells, visionary, change-maker, and steward of legacy. I am a life balance mentor for women leaders. And I know how you feel!

A veterinary pathologist and toxicologist, I left the corporate world in 2002 after 13 years of working at companies in the U. S. and France. I built a multi-six figure pre-clinical safety consultancy in Paris in less than two years, doing work that I loved. My husband and I co-founded a travel planning service in 1999, which we built alongside.

My consultancy was decimated during the 2008-2009 recession, and I re-invented myself as a productivity expert for my industry. The customized training series that I developed generated rave reviews and repeat business but not nearly enough to replace the revenue that I earned as a scientist.

I was afraid to admit that business was terrible and felt increasingly uncomfortable selling to my peers. I felt that I had no one to confide in, no one who would understand my doubts and fears. I was afraid to be viewed as a failure and worried that talk about my situation would be used against me in the industry.

As the recession deepened, I turned to a new target market – women working alone / working at home – and quickly hit a brick wall. The "know-like-trust" factor that made me attractive as a pre-clinical safety professional was non-existent in this new market, and I learned that I knew next to nothing about marketing or sales.

It was difficult to build a new skill set, create a new network, and, most importantly, rebuild my confidence. But because of my introverted nature and the job market, which would not allow me to return to the corporate world, I had to find a way to make things work.

Once again, *I found myself feeling isolated.* My old network of pre-clinical safety colleagues couldn't relate to my new activities, and my new network of transformational women entrepreneurs couldn't relate to the deep reticence I felt about possibly giving up pre-clinical safety for good.

Despite a Rolodex full of business cards and thousands of social media connections, *I felt like an outsider – **like nobody "got me."*** And I spent a couple of years and thousands of dollars searching for a mentor who understood and would advise me based on my entire professional profile, not just one of my businesses. I know firsthand what it's like to be a consummate professional who is facing challenging circumstances and feel that there's no one you can turn to for advice or even true understanding!

So, based on my hard-earned personal experiences and the mentoring that I've done over the years, I'm pleased to share a 5-step strategy that you, a high-achieving woman leader, can use to negotiate life success on your own terms.

STEP NO. 1: BE UTTERLY SELFISH

I'm sure you've heard the security announcement regarding oxygen masks that's made before takeoff aboard all airlines:

> "Please secure your own mask before assisting others ..."

To help others in this situation, you need to help yourself FIRST. Yet, women are programmed to believe that putting "self" first – being selfish – is almost sinful. That's because the word "selfish" is wed to the idea that you don't or can't care about others when you care about yourself.

Here's a news flash:

*Taking your own needs into consideration and acting on them is **the best form of selfishness.***

It benefits everyone around you – not only because you are better able to take care of others when you are whole and strong, but also because you eliminate the need to have others take care of a physically ill or emotionally feeble version of you.

Case Study #1

Melanie Patterson is a certified business advisor and coach. When we met, she was struggling to fill her client roster with start-up and emerging entrepreneurial business owners. She was doing all the "right things" but was not getting much traction building her own business, even as she was helping others achieve great results in theirs.

Additionally, she was dealing with family challenges that required a significant amount of her time and emotional energy.

Melanie dreaded working on Mondays. When she casually mentioned this one day, I asked her, "What's the worst thing that can happen if you don't work on Mondays?" She couldn't answer the question!

Melanie and I looked at the root cause of why she wasn't growing her business: she wasn't setting the boundaries required to keep things on track and always put her own needs at the bottom of her priority list.

We set up some new boundaries so she could reserve Mondays as a personal day. This alone was enough to get her to awaken refreshed and renewed every day.

Melanie told me that taking Mondays off was one of THE soundest business decisions she ever made. It increased her productivity, gave her greater peace and confidence in what she could achieve in her business, and opened time to do things like puttering in her garden that she had "back-burnered" for months.

STEP NO. 2: BE LAZY

Do any of the following statements describe you?

- You feel that you need to work twice as hard as others to maintain your current level of success and rise to the next level of accomplishment you seek.
- You have little patience with long learning curves – you expect to "get things right" the first time.

- You believe that you should always finish what you start – otherwise, people won't take you seriously.

If so, then I invite you to give yourself a break and BE LAZY for a change! The world won't stop turning if you allow yourself some time to relax. It's time for you to create space for regular self-reflection and self-care and do the inner work that will allow you to feel comfortable doing so.

When you accomplish this, you'll feel *EMPOWERED AND FREE!*

<u>STEP NO. 3:</u> Q-TIME – Quiet time to focus on you

Here's what you're missing that's keeping you from achieving your ideal lifestyle:

- Clarity
- Mindfulness
- Gratitude
- Accountability
- Celebration

The way to accomplish these things is as simple as taking time to focus on you. When you carve out precious **Q-Time** (Quiet Time) to **exhale, relax, and turn your attention inward**, you'll be able to release physical and emotional energy drains, re-evaluate your priorities, and decide what you want to change in your life. You can then create a plan to make that change a reality and set up a mechanism to hold yourself accountable for your progress.

<u>Case Study #2</u>

Vada Kornegay is an architect with many passions. When we began working together, she had several business projects and personal goals competing for her attention, and found that her personal goals were suffering as a result. She felt that she needed to define a strategic plan to move forward with all aspects of her life. Her overarching goal was to achieve *CLARITY.*

After Vada took an unflinching look at her personal priorities regarding self-care, time with family, community service, and spiritual life, we created a **master plan** for her business activities. She leveraged our weekly accountability calls for additional clarity as she moved forward, continually re-evaluating which things were most important to accomplish and the time frame for doing so.

Among her BIG WINS, she...

1) – took her teenaged daughter on a *mother-daughter vacation.*
2) – *fired an employee* who was not performing well and was increasingly resistant to training.
3) – *found a new permanent care physician* for herself.
4) – *made a decision* about a significant financial business investment.

Now, Vada does nothing without creating a strategic plan based on consideration of her life's *PURPOSE and PASSION*, paying attention to personal as well as professional goals.

STEP NO. 4: FOLLOW YOUR INTUITION

You have inner voices that are always talking to you. Some are fearmongers – they are the source of "imposter syndrome" and may make you feel that you need to "wear a mask," to pretend to be someone you are not. They come from your EGO.

Others are often soft-spoken and gentle. They may even choose not to speak at all, but rather to "message you" through physical sensations. They come from your INTUITION.

If you're so busy that you're operating on auto-pilot most of the time, you're likely not tuned into your intuition. You may have even forgotten that you have one!

Here's a personal story about how ignoring your intuition can get you into trouble!

<u>Case Study #3</u>

For my travel service's first culinary excursion, we partnered with a travel agency in the U.S., which subcontracted the marketing for the offering.

I woke up in the middle of the night with a clear message that we were not going to enroll enough people in the program to make it financially feasible. I ignored the message, thinking that it was *irrational* – surely, I would be notified if there were a problem.

I did not contact the partnering service and learned only a few days before the event that not enough people were registered. I had to scramble to get people who live in Paris to purchase spots in the program.

Things ended up working out okay, but I suffered severe anxiety during the days it took to drum up the local participants. I savagely reproached myself for not having paid attention to my *gut feeling* that something was wrong!

STEP NO. 5: INVEST IN YOURSELF

I'll bet you have no problem spending money to increase your skills and expertise or to expand your network. But when was the last time you invested in yourself *to shift a mindset or behavior that no longer serves you, to establish a new way of BEING for yourself?*

Do you have a MENTOR?

Without this type of support, you're likely to continue:

a. ... living on *auto-pilot*
b. ... *hiding* behind your mask
c. ... feeling *overwhelmed*
d. ... ignoring your *stress-related symptoms*
e. ... feeling *guilty*
f. ... *settling for less* than what you really want in life

Case Study #4

Emmanuelle Champaud is the President and CEO of TOTEM-Mobi, an entrepreneurial business that provides electric rental cars in the south of France. When we met, she was seeking guidance on many aspects of her business so she could find a partner that would move TOTEM from start-up to growth phase.

Emmanuelle was overwhelmed because she found herself unable to say *"no"* to any request and was *extremely fatigued* due to working nights and weekends for months on end. Because she was frequently doing things unrelated to her business, she wasn't focusing her attention on the work required to make it attractive to an investing partner.

We worked together on the root cause of her fatigue – doing too many non-business-related tasks and ignoring self-care. We also looked at her business mission, goals, and everyday to-dos to ensure that everything was *aligned* and moving her toward her goal.

After only two sessions with me, along with using my system for reflecting on goals, milestones, and priorities, Emmanuelle was able to articulate her business goal more clearly than ever. She decided on a strategy, implemented it, and successfully negotiated a merger that quickly transformed her business.

I love watching women uplevel their mindset and actions so they can achieve their dreams, and I love being a catalyst for their breakthroughs!

I hope you find that the 5-STEP strategy I've shared provides you with a roadmap for

— greeting every day with a new sense of passion, power, and purpose
— handling challenging situations with ease and grace
— increasing your impact and influence as a leader

When you embrace it, you are able to negotiate *life success on your own terms.*

Better yet, you'll be able to go to sleep in peace and wake up in joy!

About Dr. Monique

Dr. Monique Y. Wells is a visionary, a change-maker, and a steward of legacy. She is a native of Houston, Texas and a 28-year resident of Paris, France. Through her entrepreneurial work as a veterinary pathologist and toxicologist, travel professional, writer, speaker, and mentor, she embraces and harnesses the power of education to change lives.

Monique worked for 13 years in the corporate world before combining her passion for life sciences, literacy, STEAM (science, technology, engineering, arts, and mathematics) education, the arts, travel/study abroad, and women's empowerment under the umbrella of her U.S. non-profit organization, the Wells International Foundation (WIF).

She is also co-owner of Entrée to Black Paris (ETBP, formerly known as Discover Paris!) – a travel business that has provided services tailored for the African-American travel market since 1999. Over the years, she has created Afrocentric itineraries, self-guided and guided walking tours, a comprehensive Black Paris bus tour, and Afrocentric and other culinary activities for those wanting an in-depth, unconventional travel experience in the City of Light. Her "Paris: An Afrocentric Perspective" course is the only continuing education training for travel professionals on the African diaspora in Paris.

Because of her activities to promote and expand the legacy of painter Beauford Delaney as president of the French non-profit association, Les Amis de Beauford Delaney, Monique included the Arts as a Strategic Focus Area for WIF. Delaney was an African-American expatriate who spent the last 26 years of his life in Paris. Monique's successes in extending his legacy include the preservation of his gravesite, installation of two commemorative plaques in Montparnasse, the area where Beauford lived during most of his Paris years, and the organization of a major monographic exhibition of his work in Paris.

Through her travel business, Monique has worked with study-abroad groups across the United States since 2001. WIF and Entrée to Black Paris have welcomed women undergraduate and graduate student study-abroad interns to Paris for several years.

Monique is a three-time book author as well as a freelance journalist and editor. She is the author of the award-winning cookbook, *Food for the Soul—A Texas Expatriate Nurtures Her Culinary Roots in Paris,* co-author of *Paris Reflections: Walks through African-American Paris,* and author/ publisher of the Amazon-bestselling e-book, *Black Paris Profiles.* She has written articles for publications including the *International Herald Tribune, San Francisco Chronicle, Los Angeles Times,* and *France Today.*

In 2013, Monique was the first recipient of the Tannie Award for Excellence and Achievements in the field of Websites, Blogs, and IT for her Entrée to Black Paris™ blog. Since 2016, she has been honored to serve as the U.S. Ambassador and Delegate for France's Academy of Culinary Art for the Creole World.

A consummate storyteller and presenter of topics ranging from toxicologic pathology to life balance, Monique has addressed audiences on four continents. She has mentored women entrepreneurs on productivity and life balance and recently launched a life balance mentoring service for women leaders.

You can connect with Monique at:
- monique@moniqueywells.com
- https://www.linkedin.com/in/mywparis/
- www.twitter.com/wellsint
- www.facebook.com/EntreetoBlackParis

CHAPTER 21

LIFE-LONG LEARNER

BY WILLIAM F. NAZZARO

There are numerous elements behind success, but the most important is the ability to grow and learn throughout one's career. To paraphrase Warren Bennis and Bert Nanus, they said, "It is the capacity to continually develop and improve one's skills that distinguish leaders from followers." I wish I had realized this much earlier in my career.

At the age of 28, I finally finished my Master's in Computer Science from Rensselaer Polytechnic Institute. It was a long six years. I was going to school at night while balancing a 40+ hour workweek at Pratt & Whitney. I only took one course per semester; this allowed me to balance schoolwork with the demands of being a young software engineer.

After graduation, my parents asked if I was going to continue my education, maybe consider getting a doctorate or an MBA. I emphatically said, "No, I'm done!" Besides, what should I study, and how would I structure or organize my studies if I was done with school?

I made several job changes and eventually found myself working at a company as the Director of Software Architecture. When I started my job, I was clear with the Chief Technology Officer that I wanted to be an individual contributor who solved software problems. I just wanted to own our product's software architecture.

Over the next five years, I was given increasing responsibilities and slowly drifted away from my passions. I was no longer the Director; I was now the Vice President of Product Development and had a considerable number of people reporting to me (at one time, it was well over 100 people).

What a divergence. Only years earlier, I was adamant about being an individual contributor. But this was what they needed me to do, and I loved working for the company. Then in 2005, I was caught up in a changing of the guard and was unceremoniously let go.

I told myself, 'Well, I should be OK. I never really wanted this role in the first place. I'll just get a new job doing what I love.' Unfortunately, it wasn't that easy.

Why? Because over the past five years, I had let my technical skills erode. I was now unemployed, married, with two girls under the age of four, less than two months reserves to pay my bills in the bank, and a resume that generically read, "builder and leader of high performing teams."

I thought, 'How could this have happened to me? Only several years earlier, I was the upcoming star. And now I'm unemployed with a lack-luster resume.'

Over the next few months, through considerable reflection, it dawned on me, and I finally said, 'How could *I have LET* this happen?'

So, why do so many of us stop learning after we leave high-school, college, or post-graduate studies? Why don't we make continuing education and growth a priority? Why don't we intentionally manage our careers? How many of us are expecting our employer to give us direction? Why are so many of us **NOT** life-long learners?

As I searched for answers, I realized I hadn't taken 100% responsibility for my life, career, and personal growth. To put it bluntly – life happened. I got married, bought a house, started to have a family, and began climbing the corporate ladder.

If you have given away the responsibility for your career, personal growth, or being a life-long learner, I'd like to offer you the following. It takes intentionality of time and resources as well as a shift in mindset to re-awaken the dormant learner that lies sleeping within you.

MODEL FOR INVESTING YOUR TIME AND MONEY

The challenge many of us face is how to invest our time and money properly?

I could be a life-long learner and focus my time and money to acquire or perfect skills, but if I didn't know what my intention was with that newly-acquired or perfected skill, it could be a waste of time or at best a hobby.

I could also invest my time pursuing skills that companies or clients need, but I don't know if this could lead my career to a dead-end, or will I be fulfilled doing this type of work?

To help navigate these difficult questions and provide a visual for our decision making, see **Figure 1: Interests | Needs – Venn Diagram** *(at the top of the following page).*

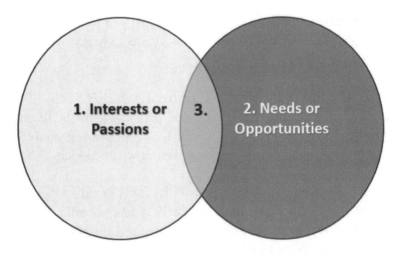

Figure 1: Interests | Needs – Venn Diagram

1. Interests or Passions

What are your interests or passions? What do you love to do or learn? These are good questions to help you think about this region. I call this the "Personal Fulfillment" region. Why? Because you are identifying things that bring you joy or excite you.

You can invest your time and money in this region, but you aren't guaranteed a monetary return on your investment. The best-case scenario is you invest in developing your interests or passions and find there is a market, but the worst case can be you invest and realize there isn't a company or client willing to pay for those skills.

Sometimes we confuse our interests and hobbies. Hobbies bring us joy. Golf is a hobby of mine, and I enjoy playing it, but unfortunately, no one is going to pay me to play golf. So, I am not talking about hobbies. I am talking about finding and investing in the development of a skill that you believe is marketable, and you can make money from it.

2. Needs or Opportunities

What are companies hiring for? What are clients buying? Is there an unfilled need or opportunity? These are just a few questions to help orient you in this region. I refer to this as the "Company Focus" region. Why? Because this represents what companies want their employees to focus on when developing their skills.

Investment in this area isn't bad. You just need to understand what it means if you grow your skills only based on your current company's or client's needs. It will help you while you're working with them, but it may not be helpful when you go to a different company. It may also be something that you aren't interested in or find fulfilling.

For example, in the late 80s and early 90s, I was a Cobol, Mainframe software developer. There was a great deal of work available to fix the Y2K problems, and I could have been busy for several years doing this work, but I wasn't passionate or fulfilled by it. I wanted to grow into an up-and-coming language at the time called Java.

I think this region can be hard, because you believe you are doing the right thing by developing in areas the company is asking for, and you feel you are a good team player, but you could be letting your skills erode.

3. The Intersection of Interests with Needs

What are you interested in or passionate about, and what are companies or clients indicating they need?

In **Figure 1: Interests | Needs – Venn Diagram**, this intersection is labeled with a "3". I call this the "Joyful Employment" region. This region represents where your interests or passions slightly overlap with the company's or client's needs or opportunities. This intersection can serve you well. However, as you look at the Venn Diagram in Figure 1, you'll notice that it's a smaller overall area.

If you find something that you are passionate about AND there is a need for it, that could be an excellent place to invest your time and money to grow those skills. Many of us have found fulfillment and employability by staying in this region.

For example, I've been passionate about helping companies streamline their software development processes and accelerate their product development for the last decade. This is something that many Fortune 500 companies have expressed a need for. I've found this type of transformation work incredibly fulfilling, and it has been a good investment on my part.

This is a good region to be in, but if you stay it and don't continue as a life-long learner, you may eventually let your skills erode and miss an opportunity.

So, what else should you be learning? What should you master? Ask yourself, if I lost my job this Friday, would I have marketable skills that could land me a fulfilling, new job?

To answer these questions, I'd like to introduce **Figure 2: Interests | Needs | Trends – Venn Diagram**. This diagram, *at the top of the following page*, is slightly modified from Figure 1. I've added a third circle entitled: "Trends or Horizon."

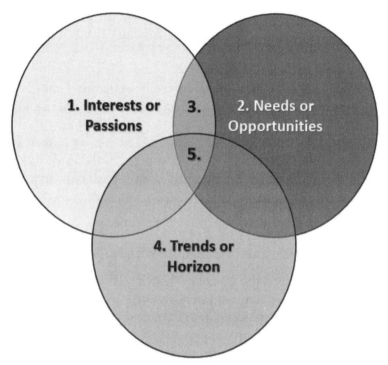

Figure 2: Interests | Needs | Trends – Venn Diagram

4. Trends or Horizon

I call this the "Big Surf" region. Why? Because when I'm looking for trends, it's similar to trying to surf a wave in the ocean. What waves are coming? Can you see those small ripples coming in the distance? We need to watch the surf so we can start paddling before that wave is actually upon us. Otherwise, it may be too late, and you'll miss the wave.

Sometimes the waves will fizzle out before they get to us. Sometimes we don't start paddling early enough to catch the wave, and the wave passes us. And sometimes we get on the wave and then we need to get off of it as it nears the shore.

Trends are like waves. We must always be on the lookout for them. Sailors have a saying, "You should never turn your back on the ocean, or you'll get caught off guard." We can never turn our backs on trends. We must always be looking for the next wave that's coming.

The hard part is we can invest in something that looks promising, but it doesn't catch on as we thought it would.

For example, I thought clients would be very interested in Service-Oriented Technology back in the early 2000s. Although I made a considerable investment in acquiring those skills, clients never really seemed to be asking for them.

5. The Intersection of Interests with Needs and Trends

This region is the "Magic" region. If you come across something that you are interested in, companies are asking for, and it's a new trend, that's when you invest heavily.

For example, I've been passionate about helping grow aspiring and emerging leaders for the last decade. This is also something that many companies have also expressed a need in, so it's something that is both fulfilling for me, and it's an excellent investment to make.

BECOMING A LIFE-LONG LEARNER

Now that I've shared guidance on how to invest your time and money, let's talk about three essential rules to establish yourself as a life-long learner.

1) Put Your Ego Aside and Be Curious

Eric Allen said, "Everyone is my teacher." When I first heard that, I thought, what a beautiful philosophy. Do you treat the world as everyone is your teacher, and you're the student? At your core, are you teachable? What does it take for you to put that ego aside and be curious about what you can learn from others?

As a consultant, I find this to be very difficult for many clients that I've worked with, and this is something I'm struggling with continually.

Several years ago, I was attending a class in which the instructor asked us to fill out our name tents but asked for something slightly different than what we are accustomed to. He asked to put in the upper right corner of our name tent, from a scale of 1 to 5 (5 being the highest) what our current level of proficiency was in this particular field of study.

We all sheepishly looked around the room to see what others were putting on their name tents. We had quite the varied responses. Some people wrote 2s, 3s, and 4s, and some even wrote down 5s.

I thought about it and wrote: 5 Trending to 1.

As we introduced ourselves, he asked me to explain my answer. I said I had a high-level of proficiency, but as I learned more, I realized I still had much to learn. So, I expected by the end of the week that I would be a beginner because my understanding of the topic will have changed and grown larger.

I reiterate, are you teachable? Or do you believe you can only learn from some people and not from others? If so, let your ego go and remain curious.

2) Be Intentional

Personal growth doesn't happen on its own. John Maxwell says, "Growth requires intentionality; it requires a plan, and it takes work."

When we were in our secondary education, college, or post-graduate work, we followed a syllabus that was defined for us by those institutions. But when we entered the workforce, we were faced with following the direction set forth by our employer or having to chart our own path. For many, this can be an under-developed skill, and having this responsibility can make us nervous.

I challenge you, don't abdicate the growth and direction of your career. Jim Rohn said, "If you don't design your own life plan, chances are you'll fall into someone else's plan. And guess what they have planned for you? Not much."

3) Start Now

An old Chinese proverb says, "The best time to plant a tree was 20 years ago. The second-best time is now." When should you start becoming a life-long learner? Now!

What can you do today? What's the smallest step you can take? To paraphrase Martin Luther King Jr., "Take the first step. You don't have to see the whole staircase; just take the first step." You don't need to see the whole path charted out ahead of you before you take action.

Remember, over time, your interests will change, your employer's or client's needs will change, and trends will change. Therefore, don't worry about having an imperfect plan. Start doing something today and then adapt.

SUMMARY

We all have seasons of our lives that can influence our priorities. When I was in my 20s, I wanted to change the world, in my 30s, I wanted fame and fortune, in my 40s, I wanted to a build a successful consulting practice, and in my 50s, I want to be the best version of myself while helping to build the next generation of leaders. Who knows what I'll want in my 60s, 70s, and 80s? But I do know this – I will always be a life-long learner.

Being a life-long learner has nothing to do with age; it just influences our priorities.

If you think you are too old to learn something new, then you are. If you think it's too hard, then it is. As Henry Ford said, "whether you think you can, or you think you can't, you're right." If you think being a learner was only crucial for the early part of your career, then you may find yourself with that lack-luster resume as I had, and asking yourself, *"How could **I have LET** this happen?"*

About William

William F. Nazzaro is the co-founder of The Time to Lead Institute. He works with individuals who aspire to become recognized leaders to advance their careers and with organizations who want to improve their company's emerging leaders to increase their market performance and innovation.

William's approach is centered on his philosophy: "Leadership is not a title or a position on an organizational chart; rather, leaders are created, not born."

As a result of working with his company, people shared that they've improved their leadership skills, work relationships, levels of influence, and have greater confidence to lead themselves and others.

He is also the president of Process Synergy, LLC. A business agility company specializing in the transformation of clients' policies, processes, and practices to bring about innovation and accelerate their product delivery to market.

His down-to-earth speaking style and pragmatic emphasis on leadership development have benefited the major auto manufacturers, health-care, pharmaceutical, human resources, insurance, financial services and banking industries, and the Department of Defense.

William is a Certified Jack Canfield Success Principles Coach, a Certified John C. Maxwell Leadership Coach, and a Certified Behavior Consultant (DISC). He has earned his B.S. in Information Technology from the University of Scranton and an M.S. in Computer Science from Rensselaer Polytechnic Institute.

He lives in Collegeville, PA, with his wife Patty of 24 years and their two daughters Athena and Angela, who are both attending college. He is an avid golfer who has played in several Pro-Ams, a roller-coaster enthusiast, and his family fosters puppies to be placed as guide dogs for The Seeing Eye®.

You can connect with William at:
- bill@timetolead.com
- bill@process-synergy.com
- www.timetolead.com
- www.process-synergy.com
- www.linkedin.com/in/williamnazzaro
- www.facebook.com/groups/yourtimetolead

CHAPTER 22

THE ICE PRINCIPLES

BY SHAWN M. COLE, M.D., M.S., M.H.A.

Realizing your own potential and investing in your personal and professional journey can be challenging and time-consuming, but finding your authentic smile is just a moment away.

My journey began on the ice at the age of five. Growing up in the Northeast, a small town in Connecticut, where ice hockey maintains high popularity, and parents usually start kids on a team at a young age. Two years after developing basic skills under the tutelage of my clinic coaches, I found myself on a travel team; hockey became a solidified aspect of my identity. I knew I was not the biggest or the strongest, but if I could solve how to become one of the smartest and the fastest, and learn to train smart and efficiently, I would optimally reach my goals of becoming an important member of my team.

As my talent began to evolve, so did my appreciation for the work ethic required to meaningfully navigate through this journey. Understanding what it means to be on the team and the responsibility you have for not only yourself but for others, became a facet of the experience that has since resonated to my core. I vividly recall the preparation required before each practice and game: my equipment needed to be aired out, jerseys washed, bag prepared, sticks taped, water bottle set out, all while preparing mentally and physically, ensuring proper rest, setting the alarm, etc. Once the team arrived at a game, our focus was playing a clean game while demonstrating sportsmanship, and of course, assuming the win with a smile. These experiences served as the foundation of my ICE principles for executing my goals and ambitions. An inner fire was ignited on a frigid ice rink surface. Little did I know at that time that this structured mentality would serve as a blueprint for crafting my purpose and callings in life.

SUCCESS IS A VERB!

What is success? It is plausible that my definition and your definition of this endpoint differ substantially. Success is challenging to measure in ways that truly define our purpose. Sure, leading the company in sales or making a million dollars represent metrics that mean the world to many of us, however, does this really assume lasting fulfillment? I believe in setting many goals and accomplishing them systematically. Pure happiness and impenetrable self-esteem will always triumph and should guide us in our daily interactions with others. The term success should not be limited to a fixed concept, but as a verb that depicts the actions and energy put forth into achieving desired outcomes where true joy is derived! The win is in the learning.

STEP OUTSIDE YOUR COMFORT ZONE!

I have the sincerest gratitude for my mentors and colleagues who taught me not only how to be a clinically sound physician, but who helped me realize that I can have a greater impact on my patients and my passion for healthcare access, by becoming a leader. It was assumed that I would enjoy patient care and mentoring medical students and residents. However, the decision to step outside of my comfort zone and become a leader amongst colleagues who possessed a level of talent and experience that surely exceeded what I could bring to the table was a pivotal moment in my journey. Through many clinical and academic positions, my learning curve was steep and fast-tracked. The only choice was to assume the position and its roles and excel in this intimidating arena. One could almost hear my inner monologue: "discover, absorb, stay humble, and hone your own leadership style now."

Was I alone in my assessment of the current state of physician-well-being which seemed severely compromised? Were the expectations unrealistic, or was it me? Attend school for seven years and then persevere through three rigorous years of medical residency required to become a practicing physician, be a positive-minded leader, maintain excellent professional credentials, pursue academic recognitions, achieve the highest level of patient satisfaction and clinical outcomes while seeing your patients for less than 15 minutes? Never make a mistake, get married, have kids, be a model father, husband, son, and member of society? Be mindful of saying what you're thinking, attend multiple meetings with no clear purpose in sight, watch costs carefully, and turn over beds quickly. Essentially, be "on" twenty-four hours a day.

Perhaps the system was set up to inhibit the original goals it had set out to accomplish, but I will leave that topic for another time. Through refocusing on my love of medicine, passion for leadership, and coaching, my journey led me to telemedicine. I found myself being confronted with numerous groundbreaking opportunities that ultimately led the virtual health space, where my team and I have been able to make a markedly greater impact on helping define its evolving applications in healthcare.

HELP IS ON THE WAY!!!

One of the most alarming realities of healthcare is the startling proportion of physicians who would never start over in pursuit of a career in medicine if they had the option to press rewind. What starts as a professional "calling" for many of my colleagues becomes less enjoyable as time passes for numerous reasons including, but not limited to, professional fatigue, escalating administrative bureaucracy, lack of adequate peer support, and fear of speaking up to help generate much needed micro- and macro-level systemic change. My passion for helping others never wavered, but faith in the system I once longed to be a part of did.

The rates of physician suicide and dissatisfaction were, and are, staggering. The secret was out. The danger was real, not only for healthcare providers but for their patients, loved ones, colleagues, and communities. Reflecting on this truth had me thinking. How many things had I abandoned over the years? From playing the guitar, traveling, or simply seeing my favorite niece and nephew. To where had my quality of life disappeared and how could I find it for my colleagues and me…fast!

Longing to help, there was only one solution. Remove myself from the toxic environment and utilize my leadership skills to influence and drive positive change. Much like on the ICE, sometimes you just need to get off the ICE and rest up for your next shift. The immediate challenges proved best left for the next line.

It is riskier to stay in a position where you are not happy. There are innumerable opportunities waiting out there for all of us. Now, more than ever, our culture or possibilities are endless. As a physician, I could work from anywhere. Manifest your possibilities with a determined mindset, and the universe will answer, but whatever you do, remember not to settle!

BE INTERPROFESSIONAL

Drawing from my great appreciation as an athlete and coach, the aspects of clinical medicine towards which I gravitated was through teaching and working as an interprofessional team towards improving patient outcomes. This advanced to leadership opportunities to teach medical residents and nurse practitioner fellows, alongside numerous other medical and behavioral trainees, to systematically learn how to collaborate with an aim to provide the highest level of patient-centered care for our nations' veterans, which has blossomed into a clinical care model that is widespread throughout the U.S. Veterans Affairs Health System. These experiences have permanently underscored the importance of leading a team, learning from others, and applying evidence-based concepts to deliver the highest quality care. As was taught to me in youth hockey, it is imperative to check your ego at the door, remaining open to learning from each and every team member, leader, patient, or customer.

AVOID THE FEAR VIRUS

Your inner voice is invariably louder than what is being said to you or the noise in the background. Condition this process and learn to mindfully activate automated negative thoughts in a way that allows your body to recognize them briefly and then quickly show them the door.

In the workplace and hockey rink, I have regretfully and commonly-witnessed ethical fading, where at the onset of their tenure, leaders of an organization initially set out to represent its mission, vision, and values, which over time has slowly eroded in favor of preserving self or financial interest. Be mindful not to align with these individuals and organizations. By contributing to these unhealthy environments, you will certainly blunt the possibility of overall growth and purpose. Striving towards maintaining a sound personal and professional moral compass will lead to genuine fulfillment and happiness, and fosters a collaborating and safe-team environment.

YOU ARE WINNING, OR YOU ARE LEARNING

One of the four noble truths of Buddhism is the truth of suffering. There is not an individual who has ever lived that did not endure the human experience of suffering. No athlete, executive, teacher, or coach has been undefeated in life! Even a world champion boxer or Olympian with a perfect record has endured injuries and moments of "defeats." While painful, these opportunities represent some of life's greatest blessings. There is not a moment along my journey where I have not been reminded that I was occasionally moving in the wrong direction. These learning opportunities are akin to the universe holding up signs leading you to a better destination. Embrace these blessings, and winning will prevail.

THE VIRTUAL POSSIBILITIES ARE ENDLESS!

I have been fortunate to blend my passion for teaching, coaching, leading, and impacting as many lives as possible through the routine application of the ICE principles. Because my heart and my senses have always been open to personal growth, even when my purpose was not as defined, a calling drew me towards situations where had I not been present, both literally and figuratively, I might have found myself less fulfilled.

My professional satisfaction has been reignited through my transition to a career as a physician leader and expert in the virtual health care industry. My impact on patient access and satisfaction has made a difference. From overseeing thousands of physicians, building evidence-based medical practices, defining new areas for industry growth, and assisting physicians and healthcare providers with understanding how to re-discover their passion for patient care, clinical leadership or simply life in general—admittedly while enjoying family, recreational activities, hobbies, community service, travel, meditation and/or prayer...the possibilities are endless. The ability to replenish is necessary to be *successful*, and it gives me the greatest satisfaction to contribute to others who are interested in practicing with a purpose and exploring new dimensions of themselves.

Nothing, and I mean nothing, can derail you from achieving your goals and happiness... well, except for you. Put into the universe what you would like out of your life and make decisions that will get you there. Apply some of the ICE principles, surround yourself with like-minded individuals, read, learn, meditate, pray, and find your happiness. Lace-up those skates and go enjoy the game of your life! Almost forty years later, taking the ICE still makes me smile, and I feel like I am just getting started.

While my journey and passions never manifested towards becoming a professional athlete, my desire to excel at new activities and ventures was evident. Whether applying these ICE principles in the hockey rink or in the martial arts dojo, discovering the immense rewards of coaching, or attending medical school and becoming a board-certified internal medicine physician and ultimately a leader, the formula was the same. Although collective experiences helped refine the mentality and formula needed to structure this mindset, the backbone of the ICE principles and gratitude for the people who have helped me achieve has remained a constant.

About Dr. Cole

Shawn M. Cole, M.D., M.S., M.H.A., is the owner and president of several national medical groups. He works extensively with physicians and other professionals, coaching them to help them realize their potential, inside and outside of the clinic setting. Dr. Cole is Board Certified in Internal Medicine, and has a strong academic Primary Care and Urgent Care background. Following completion of his Internal Medicine—Primary Care residency training at Yale-New Haven Hospital, he enjoyed six years at the Veterans Affairs Connecticut Health System. Here, he assumed an academic primary care role, and helped lead the first nurse-practitioner fellowship in interprofessional primary care – which is now serving as a model for Veterans Affairs interprofessional healthcare delivery across the country.

Subsequently, Dr. Cole became a Medical Director for Urgent Care and Patient-Centered Medical Home in the Yale-New Haven Health System. His leadership and passion for innovative healthcare solutions led to Dr. Cole being selected as the physician champion for the health system's telemedicine initiative. This led to a career-defining, instant appreciation for a healthcare delivery modality that offers convenient patient access solutions and boosts physician satisfaction.

Dr. Cole has since become an entrepreneur, digital health innovator, investor, and national leader in healthtech, serving as an advisor for venture capital groups, health systems, clinical practices, and virtual health start-up companies. With these organizations, he collaborates in drafting evidence-based clinical guidelines, strategizing IT (Information Technology) optimizations for telemedicine practice, and in providing the training/ education for, and clinical quality oversight of, physicians and other healthcare professionals.

Dr. Cole has won numerous teaching awards because of his enthusiasm for leadership and education. He also holds master's degrees in Health Administration and in Applied Nutrition.

Outside of healthcare, he is an avid ice hockey player and coach, a lifelong martial artist, and a fitness and sports nutrition enthusiast and a guitar player. Additionally, he enjoys spending time with his family, reading, and traveling.

For more information, contact him at:
- Website: https://www.shawncolemd.com/